NORTH CAROLINA SLAVES
AND
FREE PERSONS OF COLOR

STOKES AND YADKIN COUNTIES

William L. Byrd, III
and John H. Smith

HERITAGE BOOKS
2007

HERITAGE BOOKS
AN IMPRINT OF HERITAGE BOOKS, INC.

Books, CDs, and more—Worldwide

For our listing of thousands of titles see our website
at
www.HeritageBooks.com

Published 2007 by
HERITAGE BOOKS, INC.
Publishing Division
65 East Main Street
Westminster, Maryland 21157-5026

Copyright © 2001 William L. Byrd, III
and John H. Smith

All rights reserved. No part of this book may be reproduced or transmitted in any form or by any means, electronic or mechanical, including photocopying, recording or by any information storage and retrieval system without written permission from the author, except for the inclusion of brief quotations in a review.

International Standard Book Number: 978-0-7884-1880-8

FOR JO WHITE LINN

Contents

INTRODUCTION .... **VII**

ACKNOWLEDGEMENTS .... **IX**

CHAPTER ONE **1**
   STOKES COUNTY 1
     Free Persons of Color *1*

CHAPTER TWO **79**
   STOKES COUNTY 79
     Civil Actions *79*

CHAPTER THREE **137**
   STOKES COUNTY 137
     Criminal Actions *137*

CHAPTER FOUR **145**
   STOKES COUNTY 145
     Petition Exparte *145*

CHAPTER FIVE **157**
   STOKES COUNTY 157
     Mortgage of Slaves *157*

CHAPTER SIX **163**
   STOKES COUNTY 163
     Sales of Slaves *163*

CHAPTER SEVEN **169**
   STOKES COUNTY 169
     Hiring of Slaves *169*

CHAPTER EIGHT **173**

STOKES COUNTY 173
   Weapons Permits *173*

CHAPTER NINE 175

STOKES COUNTY 175
   Coroner's Records *175*

CHAPTER TEN 177

STOKES COUNTY 177
   Miscellaneous Records *177*

CHAPTER ELEVEN 181

YADKIN COUNTY 181
   Patrol Records *181*

CHAPTER TWELVE 195

YADKIN COUNTY 195
   Sales Of Slaves *195*

CHAPTER THIRTEEN 197

YADKIN COUNTY 197
   Petition Exparte *197*

APPENDIX A 199

GLOSSARY OF LEGAL TERMS 199

TABLE OF CASES 203

CIVIL & CRIMINAL ACTIONS 203

INDEX 207

Introduction

Stokes County was formed from Surry County in 1789. It was named in honor of Colonel John Stokes, a Revolutionary War soldier. John Stokes was wounded at the Waxhaw Massacre at the time when Colonel Buford's regiment was defeated by Tarelton. Colonel Stokes was later appointed by George Washington as a judge of the United States district court of North Carolina.

Stokes County is bounded by Rockingham, Forsyth, and Surry counties, and by the State of Virginia. Germantown was the county seat until 1849. When Forsyth was formed, Germanton became part of that county. In 1851 Crawford was established as the county seat. In 1852 Crawford was changed to Danbury, and it became the county seat.[1]

---

[1] David Leroy Corbitt, *The Formation of the North Carolina Counties: 1663-1943* (Raleigh: Division of Archives and History, Department of Cultural Resources, 1950) 195-196.

Yadkin County was formed from Surry in 1850. Yadkin was supposed to have been an Indian name. Yadkin is bounded by Forsythe, Davie, Iredell, Wilkes and Surry counties. The first court was held at Dowellton. Later, Wilson became the county seat. In 1852, Wilson was changed to Yadkinville. Part of Yadkin was annexed to Forsythe in 1911 and 1922.[2]

The transcribed records in this volume were derived from originals located in the North Carolina State Archives. They are listed under the general headings as "Slaves and Free Negroes," or "Slaves and Free Persons of Color." In some cases they are listed under the headings of "Miscellaneous Records."[3]

Many of the records are torn and faded, and difficult to read. Other records are partial or fragmented. Nevertheless, every attempt has been made to transcribe the complete collection, whether partial or fragmented.

All races are represented in this volume. Interactions between Black and White are displayed on both a legal and domestic level giving the reader a vivid account of everyday life in Black and White in the Antebellum South.

Records covered in this volume Are: Free Persons of Color, Civil Actions, Criminal Actions, Petition Exparte, Mortgage of Slaves, Sales of Slaves, Weapons Permits, Coroner's Records, Miscellaneous Records, Hiring of Slaves and Patrol Records.

A glossary of legal terms and a table of cases have been included at the end of this book. Both civil and criminal actions have been included in the table of cases. Definitions for legal terms were derived from *Black's Law Dictionary*.

---

[2] Ibid, 238-239

[3] Thornton W. Mitchell, "Preliminary Guide to Records Relating to Blacks in the North Carolina State Archives," *Archives Information Circular 17* (June 1980): 3-4.

Acknowledgements

The publishing of this book would not have been possible without the courteous and knowledgeable help and skills of the staff of the North Carolina State Archives. They are always willing to go the extra mile in retrieving these old records in a prompt manner.

Stokes County

Chapter One

Stokes County

Free Persons of Color

**North Carolina State Archives
Stokes County Records
Miscellaneous Slave Records
C.R.090.928.13**

Free Persons of Color

H.G. Armfield
Delivery Bond for a Yellow Boy Gideon

N. Carolina }
Stokes County }
The Subscribers bind themselves their heirs & legal representatives to Peter Tuttle, D.S., his heirs & legal representatives in the Sum of One Hundred Dollars Subject to the following Conditions: Whereas the sd. Peter Tuttle hath this day under the authority of a Capias, directed to him by the County Court of Stokes arested & taken into possession a yellow free boy, named Gideon, formerly in the possession & keeping of H.G.

Stokes County

Armfield, and now holds the said boy in Custody in order that he may be forthcoming at the ensuing County Court of the County aforesaid; And whereas the said Tuttle hath this day surrendered the said boy Gideon into the possession of the said H.G. Armfield, now if the said H.G. Armfield, on the 13th day of June next, Surrender to the said P. Tuttle the said boy Gideon, or to the high Sherif of said County or any of his deputies, or shall faithfully Surrender him to the County Court of said County on the said Thirteenth day of said month June next which is the Commencement day of said Court then the above bond to be null & void, otherwise to remain in full force & virtue -- Witness our hands & Seals
May 26th 1842.
    Hance G. Armfield   (Seal)
    J.S. Gibson   (Seal)

****

State of North Carolina } This day Martin & Joseph Rominger brought
Stokes County } a negroe Boy before me the Subscriber who says he belongs to McKiney & that McKiney bought him of Christopher Neal, living in Clear Mount, in the State of Virginia, and says he is free & his time was sold --, These are therefore to Command you to Receive in the Public Goal, of your County, the Body of Nathan Bell as he calls himself for safe keeping, or till he legally is discharged according to law -- Given under my hand & Seal the 8th of June 1828
                                    Signed   J. Butner J.P.

In obedience to the within writ, the Sheriff of Stokes States, that the prisoner in his custody, is known by the name of Nathan Bell, He was committed on the 8th day of June A.D. 1828, by order of J. Butner J.P. (a copy of which order is hereto annexed) But whether as a runaway, or as a free Negroe under the act of 1826 to prevent migration is not Stated --, He is detained in prison, only under the order of the Justice -- and that he has said negro in Court -- in obedience to the within writ.
S. Stone Shff.

North Carolina }
Stokes County }

Stokes County

To the Keeper of the Common jail of said County

 Whereas Nathan Bell a free person of Color as is sworn to & alleged hath complained to Me on oath that he is detained in your jail without any just or legal cause therefor & contrary to his own will & hath prayed that I should grant him a Writ of Habias Corpus Whereby the cause of his detainer may be inquired into -- These therefore are to command you to have the body of the said Nathan Bell before me at my chamber forthwith together with the cause of his detainer & all papers which may be in your hands touching or concerning the imprisonment of the said Nathan Bell or by whatever other Name he may be known or described, together with this writ & have you [?] executed the same.
 Given under my hand & seal this **[Blank]** day of Oct. 1828 at Germantown in the County of Stokes.

     Thos. F. Armstrong S.C.C.
     Stokes County

State of North Carolina: To the Sheriff of Stokes County, Greeting:
 You are hereby Commanded to have the Body of Nathan Bell, a Man of Color, who suggests to us that he is unlawfully detained a prisoner in the Common jail of your County under your Custody, by whatever name he may be called, together with the day & cause of his Caption & detention before the Superior Court of Law to be held for the County of Stokes at the Court house on tomorrow at nine of the Clock A.M., there to do & receive whatsoever the said Court may consider of him in the premises: Herein fail not & have you then & there this Writ.
Witness Thomas Ruffin one of our Judges of the Superior Court of Law & Equity at Stokes County this 13th day of October 1828 under his hand & Seal.

     Thomas Ruffin (Seal)

October 13th 1828

This day Came Henry Steyer[?] Before Me Isaac Conrad one of the acting Justices of the Peace & made that he is Sick & Cannot attend as a Witness at the Present Court.

Stokes County

Sworn to before Isaac Conrad JP

Henry X Steyer
his Mark

North Carolina }
Stokes County }

    To the Honorable Thomas Ruffin one of the Judges of the Supr. Courts of Law & Equity in & for said State

    The Petition of Nathan Bell Humbly Sheweth that he is a native citizen of the State of Virginia born in the County of Fairfax in said State where his father John Bell now resides a freeman of Color, that his said father by deed of Indenture dated the 19th of Febr. last past bound him apprentice to one Christopher Neal of Alexandria in the District of Columbia, to serve him as an apprentice until the 15th Jan. 1831, by whom he was sold to one McKenzie residing in South Carolina who took him on with him as far as between Salem & the town of Salisbury in this State when your Petitioner escaped from him & in endeavoring to find his way back to the place of his birth and to his father he was taken up in the County of Stokes as a runaway Slave in the month of June last past & committed to the common jail of said County Where he has been Kept in close confinement ever since -- Being born free & being detained in jail without any legal authority therefor - having been bro't into the State without his consent & contrary to his will - He prays your Honor to grant him a writ of Habeas Corpus to be directed to the Keeper of the common jail of Stokes County commanding him to have the body of your Petitioner before your Honor at such time & place as to your Honor may seem meet & proper then & there to be dealt with according to law - And as in duty bound he will ever pray &c.

Nathan Bell maketh oath that the Matters of fact set forth in the above Petition are true

                      his
                Nathan X Bell
                    Mark

Sworn to & subscribed before me Thomas Armstrong
Clerk of the Supr. Court of Law
Stokes County - This 14th day of Oct. 1828

Stokes County

Thos. Armstrong JP

John Talbut maketh oath that he is a citizen of the State of Virginia & a resident of the County of Fairfax that he is well acquainted with Nathan Bell the Petitioner in the above Petition & Knows that he is by birth free - he is well acquainted with his father John Bell & his wife the Mother of said Nathan & that they & each of them have always been accounted & held since his acquaintance with them as free exercising & using all the privileges belonging to free persons of color in that State

John Talbert

Sworn to & Subscribed before me
the 14th Octr. 1828
Thos. Armstrong JP

****

T. Fowler

State of North Carolina }
Stokes County   } December Term 1841

Ordered by the Court that Tapley Fowler a free man of color be allowed to carry a gun &c
Test

Jno. Hill

Renew the above Order

Tapley Fowler to carry a Gun

Ordered by the Court That Tapley Fowlers (a free Man of color) be allowed to carry a gun on the plantation of J.J. Martin Esq. for Twelve months the said J.J. Martin agrees to be responsible for any Misdemeanor of Tapley Fowlers in consequence of his carrying a gun.

Sept. Term 1845

Ordered by Court that Taply Fowler a free man of Colour is permitted to carry a gun for the next 12 Months.

Stokes County

Tapley Fowler

State of North Carolina } Sept. Term
Stokes County } 1845

Ordered by the Court that Taply Fowler a free man of color be permitted to carry a gun for the next twelve months.
Test   Jno. Hill

****

Drury Pettiford

State of North Carolina } September Term 1841
Stokes County }

It is Ordered by the Court that Drury Pettiford a free man of colour be permitted to carry and use his rifle for twelve months.

Test   Jno. Hill C.C.

****

[Transcribers Note: This case involves a slave woman and her children suing for freedom based upon the fact that their ancestors were free born. This case is very extensive and includes depositions from as far away as Henrico County, Virginia.]

State of North Carolina
To Richard Allin, John Welch Esquires, Justices assigned to keep the Peace for Wilkes County, and State of North Carolina,
Know Ye, that we, reposing special confidence in your fidelity and prudent circumspection, do authorise and empower you, or any of you, that at such time and place as you shall appoint, you call and cause to come before you Reuben Suttle and him diligently examine on the Holy

Stokes County

Evangelists of Almighty God, what he may know in and about a certain matter of controversy, now at issue in our Superior Court of Law for the County of Iredell wherein Jemima Scott is plaintiff, and Joseph Williams is defendant, as well on the part of the plaintiff as the defendant, and such examination and deposition by you taken, you are to send certified and enclosed, under your hands and seals, to the next court to be held for said county, at the Court House in Statesville on the 5th Monday after the 4th in September next: and this you shall in no wise omit.

    Witness James Campbell Clerk of our said Court, at Office the 5th Monday after the 4th March in the 51st year of our Independence, Anno Domini 1827.

                   Jas Campbell   Clk.

State of North Carolina }
Wilkes County   }

    Pursuant to the annexed commission to us directed at the house of Reuben Suttle in the county of Wilkes on the 29th day of October A.D. 1827 William Davis the plaintiff's agent being present we proceeded to take the following deposition of Reuben Suttle of lawful age, who having been first sworn upon the Holy Evangelists to depose the truth the whole truth and nothing but the truth between the said parties named in the said commissions deposeth and saith as follows, to wit;

    That at some time between thirty and forty years ago he the said Reuben Suttle lived with William Lewis in Surry County, and that the said Lewis put a number of working hands under him as overseer, and that said Lewis told him that he must take part of said hands away from under his oversight and have them conveyed out of the State; and that if he did not he was afraid he would lose them.

Question by the plantiff's agent. Do you recollect the names of any of the negros that Lewis sent away?

Answer, I believe he sent away one by the name of Sillar, and one by the name of Jane Scott.

Question by the same. Do you remember one by the name of Happy and one by the name of Gabriel?

Answer No; but I recollect one by the name of Sal.

Question by the same. Do you recollect that Lewis sent away Sal?

Answer, I believe he did.

And further this deponent Saith not.

Stokes County

Sworn to and subscribed before us the day and year above written
Test Rd. Allen JP
    Jn. Walsh JP   Reuben Suttle

[Transcriber's Note: The following text is from two pages which appear to be scratch pads.]

Superior Court Law
1779
Time 5 or 6 years
84: 5--
89--10--
1804

Crisson --
To [?] after the act of binding in 1804 -- Complains --[?] bought her time -- This Davis -- 38 years --That Cresson told him he bought her time -- The paper confirms him

1804	60
1779	26
25	34

Dodge --
The declaration of the counsell -- That the counsel -- had Complained -- like feeling -- The best evidence of Colour present time that they are Slaves. To rebut this present the Declaration of [?] Witnesses -- The Defendant a Tory
The Court was not open -- That he used Mr. T. Davis
Lyter -- the first man that ever practised a fraud.
Joseph Baily -- Jin [?] dark complected -- to[?] 1771 -- more than 60 y: before -- her mother [?] claimed as a Slave -- does not know that [?] was free born -- but knows that Jin was.

Isaiah Cox -- Knew Jeny 64 -- at Cresons -- with child abt 15 or 16 -- used by Cresson as his slave -- he was born in 1761
1779
1774 1/5 Saml. Davis

Stokes County

Rt Sullivan -- 1814 & 15 overseer of Col. Williams - 45 in 1821
                                    45
                                  1776
More yellow than common   Mr. Wood

[Transcriber's Note: The following records are copies of earlier deeds that were brought forth in this case.]

James Alley & Jane Scots Bill of Sale

Know all men by these presents that I James alley of Rowan County in the province of North Carrolina for and in Consideration of the Sum of thirty pounds proclamation Money to me in hand Paid by Abraham Creson I have Bargined and Sold My Right and title and I do by these present warrant My Right and title from all person or persons whatsoever Shall Lay any Claim to the said wench and as the said Jane Says that she is free I do Not Sell her for her Life time only My Right and I the said Jane agrees to serve Abraham Creson the term of time as two honest Men Shall Judge Me to serve for thirty pounds procm. Money and My Wareing Cloaths and then to be free without some further Contract I James Alley and Jane diliver up our title by these presents as Witness our hands this 22d day of January 1778[68?] and Abraham Creson agrees with Jane for her to have Liberty to Chose one Man to arbtrate the worth of her time and [?] theother in three years from this date and the sd Creson shall Refuse so to do the Wench shall be free in four years from this date.

Thomas Alley	James Alley	(Seal)
his	her	
Abraham + Eny[?]	Jane X Scot	
(Seal)		
mark	mark	

                A Copy of a record about of old Jane Scot &C.

State of North Carolina   }

Stokes County

Surry County } At a County Court of pleas and quarter Sessions begun and held in and for said County, at the Court House in Richmond on the second Monday in May AD 1779.

Be it remembered that this term; On motion of Nathaniel Williams & Spruce McCay Esquires: It is ordered that an Habias Corpus issue to the Sheriff to bring into Court the body of Jean Scott detained in custody &C. Which is as follows Viz, State of North Carolina May Sessions 1779.

To the Sheriff of Surry County Greeting. We command you, that you have before the Justices of the County Court of pleas and quarter Sessions of said County under safe and secure conduct the body of Jean Scott, who is said to be detained in our prison under your custody together with the day and cause of her being detained (by whatsoever cause the said Jean Scott be therein charged) immediately after the receipt of this Writ, to do and receive those things which the Justices of the said Court now sitting shall then and there consider of this particular: And have you then and there this writ. Witness our hands and seals this 13th day of May 1779 and in the third year of the Independence of said State

        Jos Winston   (Seal)
        William Dobson (Seal)
        Benja. Watson   (Seal)

On return of which, said Jean Scott appeared and alledged that she was detained by Abraham Creson as a Slave when in fact she the said Jean was free born, and prays she might be set at liberty. On agreement & evidence being heard by the Court -- It is adjudged by the Court that the said Jean Scott be freed from her bondage, in which she was held; And that the said Abraham discharge her therefrom. It's further ordered that the children of said Jean be bound as orphans, towit, Sarah, Presilla, Keziah & Happy Scott be bound to John Hudspeth till they arrive to the age of eighteen years; the said Hudspeth doth agree to learn sd Servants to read spin, knit & weave; and that Jemima Scott be bound to Joseph Williams till she arrives to the age of eighteen years now aged 4 1/2 years, the said Williams agrees to learn said Jemima to read, spin, knit & weave.

    Test Jo Williams CC

State of North Carolina }
Surry County } I Joseph Williams Clerk of the Court of pleas and quarter Sessions for the County of Surry; do hereby certify that the

Stokes County

foregoing to be truly copied from the minute Docket of May Term 1779 --
In Witness whereof I do hereunto set my hand & have affixed the seal of
my office to the same this 18th day of October AD 1824
     Jo. Williams CC

       Jemima Scott Indenture   A Copy
This Indenture Made the 14th day of May in the year of our Lord Christ one thousand seven hundred and seventy nine between Joseph Winston of the County of Surry & State of North Carolina on behalf of the Justices of the said County and their successors of the one part and Joseph Williams -- Witnesses that the said Joseph Winston in pursuance to an order of the said County Court made the 13th day of May and according to the directions of the act of Assembly in that case made and provided; doth put place and bind unto the said Joseph Williams a certain child named Jemima Scott aged 4 1/2 years with the said Joseph Williams, to live after the manner of an apprentice and servant untill the said apprentice shall attain to the age of eighteen years; during which time the said apprentice her master shall faithfully serve his lawful commands, every where gladly obey; she shall not at any time absebt herself from the said masters service without leave; but in all things as a good and faithful servant shall behave towards her said master; and the said Joseph Williams doth covenant promise and agree to and with the said Joseph Winston that he will teach and instruct, or cause to be taught and instructed the said child to learn to weave, spin, nitt & read and that he will constantly find & provide for the said apprentice during the term aforesaid sufficient, diet, washing lodging and apparel, fiting for an apprentice and also all other things necessary both in sickness and in health -- In Witness whereof the parties to these presents have Interchangably set their hands and Seals the day and year first written

	Jos Winston	(Seal)
Signed Sealed & delivered	Jo Williams	(Seal)
In presence of	A true Copy	
T. Rice	Test Jo Williams	(Seal)

State of North Carolina }
Surry County   }
I Joseph Williams Clerk of the Court of pleas & quarter Sessions for the County of Surry; do hereby certify that the foregoing to be a true Copy of

Stokes County

the Indenture between Joseph Winston on behalf of the Justices of the County Court of Surry & Joseph Williams which was executed at May Sessions, AD 1779. In Witness whereof I do hereunto set my hand & have affixed the seal of my office to the same this 30th day of March AD 1827

          Jo. Williams CC
         By Joseph Williams Son D.C.

WM. Woodridge	}
to	}
Executors of	}
Hudspeth	} £100,000

Know all men by these Presents that I William Wooldridge of the County of Surry & State of North Carolina am held and firmly Stand Bound unto Gibson Wooldridge Airs Hudspeth & Joseph Williams Executrs. of John Hudspeth Esqr. Deceased in the Just and full sum of One Hundred Thousand Pounds Current Money
  Which Payment well and Truly to be made I bind myself my Heirs Executors Administrators & Assigns firmly by these Presents sealed with my seal and Dated this 15th day of May Anno Dom. 1781.
The Condition of the above Obligation is such that whereas the Court of said County sometime Past did by Indenture Bind to John Hudspeth Esqr. Decd. Two Molatto Girls Named Sall Scott & Kiziah Scott untill they should arrive to Eighteen Years of Age with Certain Obligations therein Mentioned in said Indenture, and whereas the said William Woolridge hath Agreed to take into his Care & Possession the above Named Sall & Kiziah Scott & Perform the dutys therein Incumbent Now if the said William Woolridge Shall in his Part Perform every Part and Article Mentioned that was Incumbent upon the said John Hudspeth as Master in said Indenture that then the above Obligation to be Void Otherwise to Remain in full force and Virtue In Witness whereof I have hereunto set my hand & Seal the day and date first above Written.

Signed Sealed &   }
Delivered in Presence }   William Woolridge (Seal)
John Thos. Longino
Spruce Macay

Stokes County

Mr. Joseph Williams take notice that on the 26th Day of this Inst. I Shall proceed to take the Deposition of Reuben Suttle and others at the house of Peter Wood in Surry County to be read in evidence in behalf of Jemima Scott in the Suit now Depending in the Superior Court of Iredell County Wharein Jemima Scott is Plantiff and you are Defendant if the Deposition be not taken on that Day I Shall attend at the house of Sd Suttle on the 27th of Sd month in the County of Wilkes at which times and places you may attend and Cross examine if you think proper also take notice that I Shall proceed any time after 10 oclock on either of Sd Days October 13th 1827.

Wm. Davis Agt.

N.C. Surry County } october 29th 1827 this Day Came Jubale Dobbins before me James Calloway one of the acting Justices for Said County and made oath that he Delivered a Copy of the to Joseph Williams.
Sworn to and Subscribed.
and that the Said notice was Delivered on the 14th of october.
Test
J. Callaway JP   Jacob Dobbings

Notice to take Deposit. of John Burton Jos Baily

State of North Carolina } Mr. Joseph Williams
Surry County } please take notice that I Shall proceed to take the Depositions of Joseph Bailey John Burton and Thomas Gennett and others at the Court house Tavern in the City of Richmond State of Virginia Henrico County on the first Monday in September next the third if the Depositions not taken on that Day on the fourth I Shall attend at the house of Joseph Bailey to take the Deposition of Sd Bailey and others the fifth I Shall attend at the house of John Burton to take the Deposition of Sd Burton and others and on the 6th I Shall attend at the house of Thomas Gennett to take the Deposition of Sd Gennett and others to be read in Evidence in behalf of the Decendants of Jane Scott Wharein Jemima Scott Melvina Scott and Tin[?] Scott are plantiffs and you are Defendant in the Suits now Depending in Iredell Superior Court of law at Statesville at

Stokes County

which times and places you may attend and Cross Examine if you think proper I Shall be at liberty to proceed to take Depositions any time after Eight oclock in the morning either of them Days.
July the 27th 1827   Wm. Davis Agt.

I Give Joseph Williams A Copy of The Within on The 2nd day of August 1827.

                         Tho. B. Wright Shff

Superior Court of Law
First Monday in March 1829

Surry (to wit) Lewis Williams was attached to answer Malvina Scott of a plea wherefore with force and arms he assaulted beat wounded the Said Malvina and unlawfully imprisoned her against the peace of the State to her damage five hundred dollars.

    And therefore the Said Malvina Scott by her Attorney Hamilton C. Jones complains for that whereas heretofore to wit on the first day of November 1828 at the County aforesaid the Said Lewis Williams made an assault on the Said Malvina Scott and beat wounded and ill treated her and then and there imprisoned her and kept and detained her in prison without any reasonable or probable cause for a long time to wit from Said first day of November 1828 untill the fourteenth day of November in the same year and still holds & detains her in prison against her will and other wrongs to her then and there did against the peace of the State and to her damage five hundred dollars and therefore She brings her Suit.

                         H.C. Jones Atto. for Plff.

Jesse Scott by his Next Friend J. Scott Vs. Lewis Williams [1831]
Civil Action
Stokes County, NC

                       Jesse Scott by his next friend J. Scott
                                        vs
                                Lewis Williams

Stokes County

Exemplification of Record
To Stokes Spring term 1831

State of North Carolina }
Iredell County }
    Be it remembered that at a Superior Court of Law begun and held for the County of Iredell at the Court house in Statesville on the fifth Monday after the 4th Monday of September A.D. 1830 A record was filed in said Court by the Clerk of Superior Court of Law of Surry County in the following Words to wit.

State of North Carolina }
Surry County } Superior Court of Law &c holden in & for the County of Surry at the Court house in Rockford on the first Monday in March A.D. 1829.
Be it remembered that at this term Francis K. Armstrong a deputy Sheriff in and for the County of Surry returned into our said Court a Writ which is in the following Words and figures (Viz) State of North Carolina To the Sheriff of Surry County Greeting You are hereby Commanded to take the body of Lewis Williams if to be found in your bailiwick and him safely keep So that you have him here before the judge of our Superior Court of Law at the next Court to be held for the County of Surry at the Court house in Rockford on the first Monday in March next then and there to answer Jesse Scott by his next friend Jemima Scott of a plea of trespass assault & battery & false imprisonment to his damage one hundred dollars Herein fail not and have you then & there this Writ Witness Joseph Williams Clerk of our said Court at office the first Monday of September and in the 53d year of the independence of said State, Anno Domini 1828 Issued the 14th day of November 1828.   Jo. Williams C.S.C.

Endorsed on said Writ were the following Words & figures (viz) Jesse Scott vs Lewis Williams Writ trespass AB to March 1829 Executed Tho. B. Wright Shff by F.K. Armstrong D.S. Came to hand the 13th, 1828. Tho. B. Wright Shff. by F.K. Armstrong D.S. The following is a Copy of the bond for the prosecution of said Suit (viz) We and each of us oblige ourselves our heirs &c to pay or cause to be paid unto Lewis Williams all such costs & damages as may accrue on account of the within Suits not being prosecuted with effect. Given under our hands & Seals the 14th day of November 1828.

Stokes County

	Wm. Davis	(Seal)
Witness	Jas. Davis	(Seal)
H.C. Jones	Ezra Davis	(Seal)

Accompanying said Writ in the following bond (viz)
State of North Carolina }
[Blank] County   }Know all men by these presents that We Lewis Williams and Nicholas L. Williams all of the County aforesaid are held & firmly bound unto Thos. B. Wright Sheriff of Surry County in the just and full Sum of two hundred dollars current Money of the State aforesaid to be paid unto the said Tho. B. Wright Sheriff aforesaid as such Sheriff his heirs executors administrators & assigns jointly & Severally firmly by these presents Sealed with our Seals this 15th day of November Anno Domini 1828   The Condition of the above obligation is such that if the above bounden Lewis Williams who has been Arrested by the said Tho. B. Wright Sheriff as aforesaid upon a Writ returnable to the next Superior Court of Surry County at the Suit of Jesse Scott by his next friend Jemima Scott do well and truly make his personal appearance at the next Superior Court to be held for the County of [Blank] on the 1st Monday of March next then & there to answer unto the said Jesse by his next friend Jemima Scott of a plea of trespass assault & battery and false imprisonment to his damage one hundred dollars and then & there Stand to and abide by the judgment of the said Court and not depart the Said Court without leave; And the Said Nicholas L. Williams the Security of the Said Lewis Williams well and truly discharge himself as the Special bail of the Said Lewis Williams in the Said Court, then the above obligation to be void otherwise to remain in full force and effect

Signed Sealed & delivered   Lewis Williams (Seal)
in presence of   N L Williams   (Seal)

I Tho. B. Wright Sheriff of the County of Surry do hereby assign over the above obligation and Condition to Jesse Scott the plaintiff therein named his executors and administrators to Sue for & recover agreeably to an Act of Assembly in Such Case Made and provided   Given under my hand & Seal this 26th day of Feby 1829   Tho. B. Wright Shff (Seal)

After the forgoing Suit was duly entered of Record on Saturday March 7th, 1829 it was ordered by the Court in these Causes that unless a power

Stokes County

of Attorney be filed in those Causes by Tuesday of next Court that those Causes be dismissed whereupon the Suit was continued from term to term untill March term 1830 when the defendant by his Attorney entered the following pleas /Viz/ "Guard issues Justifications" Then on Affidavit of defendants agent (which affidavit is lost or mislaid) it was ordered by his honor Joseph J. Daniel Judge that Said Suit be removed for trial to the next Superior Court of Law to be held for the County of Iredell on the fifth Monday after the fourth Monday of September 1830.

State of North Carolina } I Joseph Williams Clerk of the
Surry County } Superior Court of Law for the
County aforesaid do hereby certify the foregoing to contain two Copies of the Records & proceedings in the Suit therein housed whereof I do hereunto set my hand and have affixed the Seal of my office to the same this 9 day of October 1830 Jo Williams Clk.

Jesse Scott Vs. Lewis Williams [1830]
Civil Action
Stokes County, NC

Jesse Scott }
   vs }
Lewis Williams } Bill of Costs.

To Writ $1. Tare $1 Bond 40 Cents	$2.40
To Continuance 30 to order for removal 20	.50
To Copy of Record Seal &c $1.35	1.35
To Sheriff of Surry Executing Writ	1.00
To Clerk for removal	1.00

And the agent of the defendant came in his proper person into open Court and upon his certain Affidavit in writing by him Signed Sworn to and filed moveth the Court to remove the cause to some other County for trial which affidavit is in these words here following to wit "Joseph Williams agent for Lewis Williams Swears that he does not believe the defendant can have a fair and impartial trial in this County as a Suit of a Similar nature and depending upon Similar Testimony and which excited great interest was tried here last term He further Swears that he believes

Stokes County

influential men in the County will take an Active interest in this Case against the defendant" Upon the hearing of which Affidavit and motions it is ordered by the Court here Willie P. Mangum Esquire Judge Presiding that this Suit be removed to the County of Stokes for trial And that the Clerk of this Court transmit to the Superior Court of Stokes County on or before the first day of the next term of Said Court a Copy of the Proceedings in this Suit.

I James Campbell Clerk of the Superior Court of Law of Iredell County do hereby certify that the forgoing is truly Copied from the Records in my office In Testimony Whereof I have hereunto Set my hand and affixed the Seal of my office at Statesville the 22d day of November AD 1830.   J. Campbell Clk.

Jesse Scott   }
   vs   }
Lewis Williams } Bill of Costs in Iredell

Clerk entering Seal	$ .80
Affidavit	.40
Order for removal	.20
13 Copy Sheets	1.30
Certificate & Seal	.45
Removal	1.00
	4.15

Sally Scott by Her Next Friend J. Scott [1831]
Civil Action
Stokes County, NC

Sally Scott by her next friend J. Scott
vs
Lewis Williams
Exemplification of Record
To Stokes Spring term 1831

State of North Carolina   }
Iredell County   }

Stokes County

Be it remembered that at a Superior Court of Law begun and held for the County of Iredell at the Court house in Statesville on the 5th Monday after the 4th Monday of September A.D. 1830 A record was returned into said Court by the Clerk of the Superior Court of Surry County of which the following is a Copy to wit.

State of North Carolina }
Surry County } Superior Court of Law &c holden for the County of Surry at the Court House in Rockford on the first Monday in March AD 1829. Be it remembered that at this term Francis K. Armstrong deputy Sheriff in and for the County of Surry returned into our said Court a Writ which is in the following Words (Viz) State of North Carolina To the Sheriff of Surry County Greeting You are hereby Commanded to take the body of Lewis Williams if to be found in your County and him Safely Keep so that you have him before the Judge of our Superior Court of Law at the next Court to be held for the County of Surry at the Court House in Rockford on the first Monday in March next then & there to answer Sally Scott by her next friend Jemima Scott of a plea of trespass assault & battery and false imprisonment to her damage one hundred dollars. Herein fail not. And have you then & there this Writ. Witness Joseph Williams Clerk of our Said Court at office the first Monday in September and in the 53d. year of the independence of said State Anno Domini 1828. Issued the 14th day of November 1828.
Jo Williams C.S.C.
Endorsed on the said Writ were the following Words & figures (Viz) Salley Scott vs Lewis Williams trespass A.B. to March 1829. Executed Tho. B. Wright Shff by F.K. Armstrong DS   Came to hand 13th Nov. 1828 Thos. B. Wright Shff by F.K. Armstrong D.S. The following is a Copy of the bond for the prosecution of said Suit (viz) We and each of us oblige ourselves our heirs &c to pay or cause to be paid unto Lewis Williams all such costs & damages as may accrue on account of the within Suits not being prosecuted with effect Given under our hands & Seals the 14th day of November 1828.

	Wm. Davis	(Seal)
Witness	Jas. Davis	(Seal)
H.C. Jones	Ezra Davis	(Seal)

Accompanying said Writ is the following bond (viz)
State of North Carolina }

Stokes County

[Blank] County } Know all men by these presents that we Lewis Williams and Nicholas L. Williams all of the County aforesaid are held and firmly bound unto Thos. B. Wright Sheriff of Surry County in the just and full Sum of two hundred dollars current money of the State aforesaid to be paid unto the said Thos. B. Wright Sheriff as aforesaid as such Sheriff, his heirs executors, administrators and assigns jointly and Severally firmly by these presents Sealed with our Seals and dated this 15th day of November Anno Domini 1828. The Condition of the above obligation is such that if the above bounden Lewis Williams who has been arrested by the said Thos. B. Wright Sheriff as aforesaid upon a Writ returnable to the next Superior Court of Surry County at the Suit of Sally Scott by her next friend Jemima Scott do well & truly make his personal appearance at our next Superior Court to be holden for the County of Surry on the first Monday in March next then and there to answer unto the said Sally Scott by her next friend Jemima Scott of a plea of trespass Assault & battery & false imprisonment to her damage one hundred dollars and then and there stand to & abide by the judgment of said Court & not depart the said Court without leave; And the said Nicholas L. Williams the security of the said Lewis Williams well and truly discharge himself as the Special bail of the said Lewis Williams in the said Court then the above obligation to be void otherwise to remain in full force and effect.

Signed Sealed & delivered   Lewis Williams   (Seal)
in presence of   N L Williams   (Seal)

I Tho B Wright Sheriff of the County of Surry do hereby assign over the above obligation and Condition to Sally Scott by her next friend Jemima Scott the plaintiff therein named executor & administrator to Sue for and recover agreeably to an Act of Assembly in such case made & provided Given under my hand & Seal this 26 day of Feby. 1829 Tho B Wright Shff (Seal)

After the foregoing Suit was duly entered of Record viz on Saturday March 7th, 1829 it was ordered by the Court in those causes that unless a power of Attorney be filed in those causes by Tuesday of Next Court that those causes be dismissed Whereupon the Suits was continued from term to term till March term 1830 when the defendant by his Attorney entered the following Pleas (viz) "Guard issue justifications" then on Affidavit of

Stokes County

defendants agent (which affidavit is lost or mislaid) it was ordered by his honor Joseph J Daniel Judge that said Suit be removed for trial to the next Superior Court of Law to be holden for the County of Iredell on the fifth Monday after the fourth Monday in September A.D. 1830

State of North Carolina }
Surry County } I Joseph Williams Clerk of the Superior Court of Law for the County aforesaid do hereby certify the foregoing to contain true Copies of the records & proceedings in the Suit therein named In Witness whereof I do hereunto set my hand & have affixed the Seal of my office to the same this 9th day of October A.D. 1830
Jo Williams C.S.C.

Sally Scott }
    vs } Bill of Costs
Lewis Williams }

To Writ $1 to tax $1. Bond 40 Cents	$2.40
To 1 Continuance 30 order for removal 20	.50
To Copy of Record & Seal &c $1.35	1.35
T Shff of Surry Executing Writ $1	1.00
To Clerk for removal	1.00

And the agent of the defendant came in his proper person into open Court and upon his certain affidavit in writing by him signed Sworn to and filed moveth the Court to remove the cause to Some other County for trial which Affidavit is in these words herefollowing to wit "Joseph Williams agent for Lewis Williams Swears that he does not believe the defendant can have a fair and impartial trial in this County as a Suit of a Similar Nature and depending upon Similar Testimony and which excited great interest was tried here at last term. He further Swears that he believes influential men in the County will take an Active interest in the Case against the defendant."

Upon the hearing of which Affidavit and Motion it is ordered by the Court here Willie P. Mangum presiding that this Suit be removed to the County of Stokes for trial and that the Clerk of this Court transmit to the Superior Court of Stokes County on or before the first day of the next term of Said Court a Copy of the proceedings in this Suit.

Stokes County

I James Campbell Clerk of the Superior Court of Iredell County do hereby certify that the foregoing is truly Copied from the Records in my office In Testimony whereof I have hereunto Set my hand and Affixed the Seal of my office at Statesville the 22d day of November 1830.

J. Campbell Clk.

Sally Scott } Bill of Costs in Iredell
vs }
Lewis Williams }

Clerk entering Suit	$ .80
1 affidavit	.40
1 order for removal	.20
13 Copy Sheets	1.30
Certificate & Seal	.45
Removal	1.00
	$4.15

Malvina Scott Vs. Lewis Williams [1831]
Civil Action
Stokes County, NC

Malvina Scott
vs
Lewis Williams
Exemplification of Record
To Stokes Spring Term 1831

State of North Carolina }
Iredell County }

Be it remembered that at a Superior Court of Law begun and held for the County of Iredell at the Court house in Statesville on the fifth Monday after the fourth Monday in September A.D. 1830 before the honorable Willie P. Mangum Esquire one of the Judges of the Superior Courts of Law and Courts of Equity and presiding Judge of Said Court of Iredell County a record was filed by the Clerk of Surry County in Said Court in the following Words to wit.

Stokes County

"State of North Carolina }
Surry County } Superior Court of Law &c holden in the County of Surry at the Court house in Rockford on the first Monday in March A.D. 1829.
Be it remembered that at this term Francis R. Armstrong a deputy Sheriff in and for the County of Surry returned into our said Court a Writ which is in the following Words & figures viz

"State of North Carolina }
Surry County } To the Sheriff of Surry Greeting
You are hereby commanded to take the body of Lewis Williams if to be found in your County and him safely keep so that you have him before the honorable judge of our Superior Court of Law to be held for the County of Surry at the Court house in Rockford on the first Monday in March next then and there to answer Melvina Scott of a plea of trespass, assault & battery & false imprisonment to her damage five hundred dollars. Herein fail not and have you then and there this Writ. Witness Joseph Williams Clerk of our said Court at office on the first Monday of September Anno Domini 1828 Issued the 14th day of November 1828 Jo Williams CSC"

Endorsed on the said Writ were the following Words and figures viz "Melvina Scott vs Lewis Williams Writ trespass AB to March 1829. Executed Thomas B Wright Shff by F K Armstrong D.S. Came to hand the 13th Nov 1828 Tho B Wright Shff by F K Armstrong DS"
The following is a Copy of the bond for the prosecution of said Suit Viz "November 14th, 1828. We acknowledge ourselves indebted to Lewis Williams in the amount of all such costs & damages as shall arise from the within Suits not being prosecuted with effect. Witness our hands & Seals

	Wm Davis	(Seal)
Witness	F Davis	(Seal)
H.C. Jones	Ezra Davis	(Seal)"

Accompanying said Writ is the following bond Viz
"State of North Carolina }
S. County } Know all men by these presents that we Lewis Williams & Nicholas Williams all of the County aforesaid are held and firmly bound unto Tho B Wright Sheriff of Surry County in the just and full sum of one thousand dollars current money of the State aforesaid

Stokes County

to be paid unto the said Tho B Wright Sheriff aforesaid as such Sheriff, his heirs executors administrators & assigns jointly and Severally firmly by these Presents Sealed with our Seals & dated this 15 day of November Anno Domini 1828.

The Condition of the above obligation is such that if the above bounden Lewis Williams who has been Arrested by the said Tho B Wright Sheriff as aforesaid upon a Writ returnable to the next Superior Court of Surry County at the Suit of **[Blank]** do well and truly make his personal appearance at our next Superior Court to be holden for the County of Surry on the 1st Monday in March next then & there to answer the said Melvina Scott of a plea of trespass assault & Battery & false imprisonment to her damage five hundred dollars and then & there Stand to & abide by the judgment of the said Court and not depart the said Court without leave and the said Nicholas L Williams the Security of the said Lewis Williams well and truly discharge himself as Special bail of the said Lewis Williams in the said Court then the above Obligation to be void otherwise to remain in full force and effect

                                        Lewis Williams   (Seal)
Signed Sealed & delivered   NL Williams   (Seal)
in presence of

I Tho B Wright Sheriff of the County of Surry do hereby assign over the above obligation & Condition to Melvina Scott the plaintiff therein named her executors administrators to Sue for and recover agreeably to an Act of Assembly in Such Case made and provided Given under my hand & Seal this 26th day of February 1829. Tho B Wright Shff (Seal)

After the foregoing Suit was duly entered of Record viz on Saturday March 7th, 1829 it was ordered by the Court in these cases that unless a power of Attorney be filed in those cases by Tuesday of next Court that there Causes be dismissed, Whereupon the Suit was continued from term to term untill March term 1830 when the defendant by his Attorney entered the following pleas viz "Gen issue Justification" Then on affidavit of defendants agent (Which affidavit is lost or mislaid) it was ordered by his honor Joseph J Daniel Judge that said Suits be removed to the next Superior Court of Law to be holden for the County of Iredell on the fifth Monday after the fourth Monday in September A.D. 1830.

Stokes County

State of North Carolina }
Surry County } I Joseph Williams Clerk of Surry Superior Court of Law do hereby certify the foregoing is a true copy of the records and proceedings in the Suit therein named In witness whereof I have hereunto set my hand & have affixed the Seal of my office to the same this 8th day of October 1830.

Jo Williams C.S.C.

Melvina Scott }
    vs }
Lewis Williams } Bills of Costs

To Writ $1. tax $1. Bond 40 Cents	$2.40
To 1 Continuance 30 to order for removal 20	.50
Copy of Record Seal &c	1.35
To FK Armstrong DShff of Executing Writ	1.00
To Clk for removal	1 --

And this case coming on to be heard the agent of the Plaintiff Joseph Williams came into Court and by his certain affidavit in writing by him Signed and duly Sworn to in open Court & filed moveth the Court here to remove this Suit to some other County for trial which Affidavit is in these words to wit, "Joseph Williams agent for Lewis Williams swears that he does not believe the defendant can have a fair and impartial trial in this County as a Suit of Similar Nature and depending on Similar Testimony and which exacted great interest was tried here at last term and he further Swears that he believes influential men in the County will take an active interest in this case against the defendant"

Upon which motion and affidavit it is ordered by the Court here that this Suit be removed for trial to the Superior Court of Law of Stokes County and that the Clerk of this Court transmit a Copy of the Proceedings in this Cause to the Clerk of the Superior Court of Law of Stokes County on or before the first day of the next Session of said Court of Stokes County.
I James Campbell Clerk of the Superior Court of Law of Iredell County do hereby certify the foregoing is truly Copied from the Records in the aforesaid Suit in the office of said Court. In Testimony whereof I have hereunto Set my hand and affixed the Seal of my office at Statesville the 22d day of November A.D. 1830.

J Campbell Clk.

Stokes County

Melvina Scott	}	Bill of Costs in Iredell Supr Ct Law.
vs	}	Clerk entering
Lewis Williams	}	

.40	1 Affidavit
.20	order for removal
1.0	Removal
2.0	Copy Sheets $4.15
4.15____	

Jemima Scott Vs. Lewis Williams [1831]
Civil Action
Stokes County, NC

Jemima Scott
vs
Lewis Williams
Exemplification of Record
To Stokes Spring term 1831

State of North Carolina }
Iredell County Ss   } Be it remembered that at a Superior Court of Law begun and held for the County of Iredell at the Court house in Statesville on the 5th Monday after the 4th Monday in September A.D. 1830 before the honorable Willie P Mangum Esquire one of the judges of the Superior Courts of Law and Courts of Equity and presiding judge of said Court of Iredell County a record was filed in said Court by the Clerk of Surry County in the following Words to wit

"State of North Carolina } Superior Court of Law holden in & for
Surry County   } the County of Surry at the Court house in Rockford on the first Monday in March AD 1829

Stokes County

Be it remembered that at this term Francis K Armstrong deputy Sheriff in and for the County of Surry returned into our said Court, a writ which is in the following Words and figures viz

"State of North Carolina } To the Sheriff of Surry County Greeting
Surry County } You are hereby commanded to take the body of Lewis Williams if to be found in your County and him Safely Keep So that you have him before the honorable Judge of our Superior Court of Law to be held for the County of Surry at the Court house in Rockford on the first Monday of March next then and there to Answer Jemima Scott of a plea of trespass A.B. and false imprisonment to her damage two hundred & fifty dollars Herein fail not and have you then and there this Writ Witness Jo Williams Clerk of our Said Court at office on the first Monday of September Anno Domini 1828 Issued the 13th day of November 1828 Jo Williams CSC"
On the back of said Writ were the following Words & figures viz Jemima Scott vs Lewis Williams trespass AB Writ to Surry. Supr. Court 1828 March term Executed Tho B Wright Shff by FK Armstrong D.S. came to hand the 13th Nov. 1828, Tho B Wright Shff by FK Armstrong D.S."
The following is a Copy of the bond for the prosecution of said Suit viz "We and each of us acknowledge ourselves indebted to Lewis Williams in the amount of all such Costs and damages as may accrue from the within Suit not being Prosecuted with effect Witness our hands & Seals this 14th Novr. 1828

	Wm Davis	(Seal
Witness	J Davis	(Seal)
H.C. Jones	Ezra Davis	(Seal)

Accompanying said Writ is the following bond Viz
"State of North Carolina }
[Blank] County } Know all men by these presents that we Lewis Williams and Nicholas Williams all of the County aforesaid are held and firmly bound to Tho B Wright Sheriff of Surry County in the just and full sum of four hundred dollars current money of the State aforesaid to be paid to the said Tho B Wright Sheriff as aforesaid as such Sheriff his heirs executors Administrators and assigns jointly and severally firmly by these presents, Sealed with our Seals and dated this 15th day of Novr. Anno Domini 1828. The Condition of the above obligation is such that if

Stokes County

the above bounden Lewis Williams who has been arrested by the said Tho B Wright Sheriff as aforesaid upon a Writ returnable to the next Superior Court for Surry County at the Suit of Jemima Scott do well and truly make his personal appearance at our next Superior Court to be holden for the County of Surry on the first Monday of March next then and there to answer unto the said Jemima Scott of a plea of trespass on the Cause A.B. and false imprisonment to her damage two hundred dollars and then and there stand to and abide by the judgment of the said Court and not depart the said Court without leave; And the said Nicholas L. Williams the Security of the said Lewis Williams well and truly discharge himself as Special bail of the said Lewis Williams in the said Court then the above obligation to be void otherwise to remain in full force and effect.

                                            Lewis Williams   (Seal)
Signed Sealed and delivered   N.L. Williams   (Seal)
in presence of

I Tho B Wright Sheriff of the County of Surry do hereby assign over the above obligation & Condition to Jemima Scott the plaintiff therein named her executors & administrators to Sue for & recover agreeably to an Act of Assembly in Such Case made and provided Given under my hand & Seal this 26th day of February 1829

                                                      Tho B Wright Shff (Seal)

After the foregoing Suit was duly entered of record viz on Saturday March 7th, 1829 it was ordered by the Court in these Cases that unless a Power of Attorney be filed in these causes by Tuesday of next Court that these Causes to be dismissed whereupon the Suit was continued from term to term till March term A.D. 1830 when the defendant by his Attorney entered the following pleas viz "Gen issue justification" Then on Affidavit of defendants agent (Which affidavit is lost or mislaid) it was ordered by his honor Joseph J Daniel the Presiding judge that said Suit be removed to the Next Superior Court of Law to be held for the County of Iredell on the fifth Monday after the fourth Monday of September A.D. 1830.

State of North Carolina   } I Joseph Williams Clerk of the Superior
Surry County   } Court of Law for the County aforesaid do hereby certify the foregoing is a true Copy of the Records and proceedings in the Suit therein Named. In Witness whereof I do hereunto set my hand

Stokes County

& have affixed the Seal of my office to the same this 8th day of October A.D. 1830.

Jo Williams CSC

Jemima Scott	}	
vs	} Bill of Costs from Surry	
Lewis Williams	}	

To Writ $1.00 Tax $1 Bond 40 Cents	$2.40
To 1 continuance 30 to order for removal 20	.50
Copy of record Seal	1.00
To Shff of Surry FK Armstrong Executing Writ	1.00
To Clerk for removal	1.00

And the agent of the defendant came in his proper person and upon his certain affidavit by him Signed Sworn to and filed (the original of which is herewith Sent) Moved the Court here that that this cause be removed to Some other County for trial which affidavit is in the following Words to wit: "Joseph Williams agent for Lewis Williams Swears that he does not believe the defendant can have a fair and impartial trial in this County as a Suit of Similar Nature and depending upon Similar testimony and which excited great interest was tried here at last term And he further Swears that he believes influential men in the County will take an Active interest in this Case against the defendant" Upon the hearing of which affidavit and motion it is ordered by the Court here that this Cause be removed to the County of Stokes for trial and that the Clerk of this Court transmit to the Superior Court of Stokes on or before the first day of Next term of said Court a Copy of the Proceedings in this Suit.

I James Campbell Clerk of the Superior Court of Law for the County of Iredell do hereby certify that the foregoing is truly Copied from the proceedings in the Suit therein named In Testimony whereof I have hereunto Set my hand and affixed the Seal of my office at Statesville the 22d day of November AD 1830.

J Campbell Clk.

Jemima Scott	}		
vs	}		
Lewis Williams	} Bill of Costs from Iredell		
Clk entering the cause			$ .80

Stokes County

1 affidavit	.40
1 order for removal	.20
13 Copy Sheets	1.30
Certificate & Seal	.45
Removal	1.00
	$4.15
Wm Bunch pltffs witness	8.86

Jemima Scott Vs Lewis Williams
Subpoena for Deft.
Charles Steelmon Senr. To Spring Term 1831
Executed Thos. B. Wright shff
By E. Rutledge DS

State of North Carolina
To the Sheriff of Surry County Greeting. You are hereby commanded to summon Charles Steelmon Senr. & Samuel Speer personally to be and appear before the Judge of our Superior Court of Law, at the next Court to be held for our said County, at the Court House in Germanton on the third Monday after the 4th Monday in March next, then and there to testify, and the truth to say, in behalf of Lewis Williams in a certain matter of controversy before said Court depending, and then and there to be tried, wherein Jemima Scott is plaintiff, and Lewis Williams is defendant. And this you shall in no wise omit, under the penalty prescribed by law.
Witness Thomas T. Armstrong Clerk of our said Court, at office the third Monday after the 4th Monday of September in the fifty
[Blank] year of our Independence, A.D. 1830.

Thos. T. Armstrong Clk

Stokes Supr. Court begins the 18th of April -- Mr. Steelmon will be there on Tuesday at 10 oclock will be in time JW

Jesse Scott by His Next Friend Gemima Scott Vs. Lewis Williams
[1831]
Civil Action
Stokes County, NC

Stokes County

Jesse Scott by his next friend Gemima Scott
Vs
Lewis Williams
Commission

State of North Carolina

To **[Blank]** Esquires, Justices of the Peace for Henrico county, in the State of Virginia Greeting:
    We, reposeing especial trust and confidence in your integrity and ability, do hereby authorise and empower you to cause to come before you, at such time and place as you shall appoint. Joseph Bailey and Thomas Ginnett and them on oath examine, and their deposition in writing take, touching all such matters and things as they may know concerning a certain matter of controversy in our Superior Court pending, wherein Jesse Scott by his next friend Mima Scott plantiff and Lewis Williams defendant, and their deposition when by you so taken in fair writing upon paper, you will forward under your hand and seal, directed to the Judge of our next Superior Court to be held for Stokes County, at the court house in Germanton on the 3rd Monday after the 4th Monday in March, next, to be read as evidence on behalf of the plff.
    In Testimony whereof, I T. T. Armstrong Clerk of said Court, do hereunto subscribe my name and affix my seal of office, at Office the 3rd Monday after the 4th Monday in September A.D. 1830.
    Issued the 4th day of March 1831.

                                  Thos. T. Armstrong, Clk.

Sally Scott by Her Next Friend Jemima Scott [1831]
Civil Action
Stokes County, NC

Sally Scott by her next friend Jemima Scott
Vs
Lewis Williams
Commission
State of North Carolina

Stokes County

To Samuel Pleasants Esquire Esquire, Justice of the Peace for Henrico County, in the State of Virginia Greeting:

We, reposeing especial trust and confidence in your integrity and ability, do hereby authorise and empower you to cause to come before you, at such time and place as you shall appoint, Joseph Bailey and Thomas Gennett, and them on oath examine, and their deposition in writing take, touching all such matters and things as they may know concerning a certain matter of controversy in our Superior Court pending, wherein Sally Scott by her next friend Mima Scott is plaintiff and Lewis Williams defendant, and their deposition, when by you so taken in fair writing upon paper, you will forward under your hand and seal, directed to the Judge of our next Superior Court to be held for Stokes County, at the court house in Germanton on the 3rd Monday after the 4th Monday in March next, to be read as evidence on behalf of the Plff.

In Testimony whereof, I T.T. Armstrong Clerk of said Court, do hereunto subscribe my name and affix my seal of office, at office the 3rd Monday after the 4th Monday in Septr. A.D. 1831.

Issued the 4th day of March 1831 Tho. T. Armstrong Clk.

[Missing] to a commission to me directed [Missing] by the Honourable Superior Court of [Missing] I caused Joseph Bailey to come before me Samuel Pleasants, one of the justices of the peace for Henrico County State of Virginia, at the house of the said Joseph Bailey in the said County of Henrico on the 8th day of April 1831. And the said Joseph Bailey being first duly sworn to give evidence in the Suit pending in Said Court, Wherein Sally Scott (by her next friend Mima Scott is Plaintiff, and Lewis Williams is defendant to the several interrogatories to him proposed on his corporal oath declareth as follows towit) Present Thomas Ladd, Agent for Plaintiff.

Question by the Plaintiffs agent. Did you know a woman or Girl in Virginia by the name of Jin Scott?

Answer. I did.

Question by the same. How old was Jins Mother when you knew her?

Answer. I knew her Mother very well, but I have no distinct reccollection when she died.

Question by the same. What was Jin's age?

Answer. She was about twelve or thirteen years of age when I last saw her.

Question by the same. What was her Colour?

Stokes County

Answer. She was rather dark complected.
Question by the same. When did you last see her?
Answer. About sixty odd years ago.
Question by the same. Who was Jins Mother. Was she and her Mother Nan ever to your knowledge Claimed by any one as slaves?
Answer. Her name was Nan Scott and neither her nor her Mother was ever Claimed here by any person as slaves.
Question by the same. Were they taken and accepted as free persons?
Answer. They were considered by every person who knew them to be free persons.
Question by the same. Were they Called by the name of Scott?
Answer. They were.
Question by the same. Is John Burton dead?
Answer. I have no doubt of it from universaly report.

Joseph Bailey

Sworn to & subscribed before me this 8th day of April 1831.
                Samuel Pleasant JP   (Seal)

The Scotts Vs. Lewis Williams
Civil Action
Stokes County, NC

The Scotts Vs Lewis Williams
Notice to take Depositions

I Served a copy of this notice on Joseph Williams agent for Defendant and one copy on J.R. Dodge Atto. for Dft. both on 7th day of March 1831.
Tho. B. Wright   Shff
By E. Rutledge   D.S.

Mr. Lewis Williams
     I hereby give you notice that I expect the depositions of Joseph Bailey and Thomas Ginnett will be taken at the Court House Tavern in the City of Richmond Va on Thursday 7th of April next and if not taken on that day my agent will attend at the house of Joseph Bailey in Henrico County State of Virginia the next day towit Friday 8th for the same purpose and if not taken then & there he will attend on Saturday 9th of

Stokes County

that month at the house of Thomas Gennett in the County of Henrico State of Virginia for the same purpose In the Several cases of Mima Scott Vs Lewis Williams - Malvina Scott Vs Same Jesse Scott by his next friend Vs Same Sally Scott by her next friend Vs Same now pending in the Superior Court of Stokes County, When and where you may attend and cross examine if you think proper   Respectfully
March 7th 1831   H.C. Jones
                                                         Agent & Atto for Plffs

---

State of North Carolina

To Samuel Pleasants Esquire
    Esquires, Justices, assigned to keep the Peace for Henrico County, and State of Virginia.
    Know Ye, that we, reposeing special confidence in your fidelity and prudent circumspection, do authorise and empower you, that at such time and place as you shall appoint, you call and cause to come before you Joseph Baily and him diligently examine on the Holy Evangelists of Almighty God, what he may know in and about a certain matter of controversy, now at issue in our Superior Court of Law, for the County of Stokes wherein Malvina Scott is Plaintiff, and Lewis Williams is Defendant, as well on the part of the Plaintiff as the Defendant; and such examination and deposition by you taken, you are to send, certified and enclosed, under your hands and seals, to the next Court to be held for said County, at the Court House in Germanton on the third Monday after the 4th Monday in September next; and this you shall in no wise omit.
    Witness, Thomas T. Armstrong Clerk of our said Court, at office the 3rd Monday after 4th Monday in March A.D. 1831 and in the fifty fifth year of our Independence.
                            Tho. T. Armstrong Clk.

Pursuant to the annexed Commission to me directed by the Honourable Superior Court of Stokes County North Carolina I caused Joseph Bailey to come before me Samuel Pleasants one of the Justices of the Peace for the County of Henrico on Friday 30th day of September A.D. 1831 at the house of Said Joseph Bailey in Saide County of Henrico and he being duly Sworn to give evidence in the

Stokes County

Suit pending in Said Superior Court of Stokes Wherein Malvina Scott is Plaintiff and Lewis Williams is defendant to the Several interrogatories to him proposed the said Joseph Bailey deposeth and saith as follows.
Present Thomas Ladd agent for Plaintiff & Wray Thomas for Defendant.
Question by Plaintiff. Did you know a certain woman or girl in this County by the name of Jin Scott.
Answer. I did.
Question by same. How old was Jin when you last saw her.
Answer. She was twelve or thirteen years of age when I last saw her.
Question by same. What was her colour?
Answer. She was rather dark complected.
Question by same. When did you last see Jin?
Answer About sixty odd years ago.
Question by same. Did you know Jins Mother. What was her name and was She or Jin claimed as a Slave by anyone?
Answer. I knew her, her name was Nan Scott and neither her nor her daughter was ever claimed here as slaves.
Question by same. Were they taken and accepted as free persons by the community?
Question by same. Were they called Scott
Answer They were.
Question by same. Are John Burton & Thomas Ginnett reported to be dead?
Answer. I have no doubt of it from universal report.

Question by Defendants Agent. Have you ever seen any writing purporting to give Jin Scotts Mother her freedom or did you ever hear any one say he had seen such a writing?
Answer. I never have.
Question by the same. All that you know about the freedom of Jin Scotts Mother is that she passed in the neighborhood as a free woman of colour?
Answer. She passed as a free woman of colour.
Question by the same. You can't say that Jin Scott whom you knew sixty odd years ago is the one mentioned in this Cause?
Answer. I cant say.

Question by the Plaintiffs agent. Dont you know of your own knowledge that Nan Scott the Mother of Jin was free born?
Answer. I do not because she was older than myself.

Stokes County

Question by the same. Dont you know of your own knowledge that Jin Scott the daughter of Nan was born free?
Answer. I do.
Question by the same. Was it customary when you knew Jin Scott, and for many years after for free born persons of colour to have any free papers?
Answer. No.

        Joseph Bailey

Sworn to & subscribed before me this 30th day of September 1831.
      Saml. Pleasants J.P. (Seal)

Opened by the Clerk T.T. Armstrong
Clerk of Stokes County North Carolina

      Scott Vs Williams
     State of North Carolina

To Samuel Pleasants Esquire
  Esquire, Justice assigned to keep the Peace for Henrico County, and State of Virginia.
  Know Ye, that we, reposeing special confidence in your fidelity and prudent circumspection, do authorise and empower you, that at such time and place as you shall appoint, you call and cause to come before you Joseph Bailey and him diligently examine on the Holy Evangelists of Almighty God, what he may know in and about a certain matter of controversy, now at issue at our Superior Court of Law for the county of Stokes wherein Sally Scott by her next friend is Plaintiff, and Lewis Williams is Defendant, as well on the part of the Plaintiff as the Defendant; and such examination and deposition by you taken, you are to send, certified and enclosed, under your hands and seals, to the next Court to be held for said County, at the Court House in Germanton on the 3rd Monday after the 4th Monday in Sept. Next; and this you shall in no wise omit.
  Witness, Thomas T. Armstrong Clerk of our said Court, at Office the third Monday after 4th Monday in March A.D. 1831 and in the fifty fifth year of our Independence.
       Thos. T. Armstrong Clk.

Stokes County

Persuant to the annexed commission to me directed by the Honourable Superior Court of Stokes County North Carolina I caused Joseph Bailey to come before me Samuel Pleasants one of the Justices of the Peace for Henrico County State of Virginia at the house of said Joseph Bailey in said County of Henrico on Friday 30th of September 1831 and the sd. Joseph Bailey being duly sworn to give evidence in the Suit now pending in said Superior Court of Stokes County wherein Sally Scott by her next friend is Plaintiff and Lewis Williams is defendant to the several interrogatories to him proposed to him on his oath aforesaid reposeth and Saith as follows. Present Thos. Ladd agent for the Plaintiff and Wray Thomas for the Defendant --

Question by Plaintiff. Did you know a certain woman or girl in Henrico by the name of Jin Scott.
Answer. I did.
Question by same. What was her colour.
Answer. She was rather dark Complected.
Question by same. How old was Jin when you last saw her.
Answer. She was about twelve or thirteen years of age when I last saw her.
Question by same. How long has it been since you last saw Jin.
Answer. About Sixty odd years ago.
Question by same. Did you know Jins mother & what was her name and was she or Jin claimed by any one as slaves.
Answer. I knew her, her name was Nan Scott and neither her nor her daughter was ever claimed here as slaves.
Question by same. Were they taken and accepted as free persons by the community.
Answer. They were considered by every person who knew them to be free persons.
Question by same. Were they called Scott.
Answer. They were.
Question by same. Are John Burton & Thomas Ginnett reported to be dead and did they die in Henrico.
Answer. I have no doubt of it from universal report.

Stokes County

Question by the Defendants agent. Have you ever seen any writing purporting to give Jin Scotts Mother her freedom, or did you ever hear any one say he had ever seen such writing.
Answer. I never have.
Question by the same. All that you knew about the freedom of Jin Scotts Mother, is that She passed in the neighborhood as a free Woman of Colour.
Answer. She passed as a free Woman of Colour.
Question by the same. You cant say that Jin Scott whom you knew Sixty odd years ago is the one mentioned in this Cause.
Answer. I Cant say.
Question by the Plaintiffs agent. Dont you know of your own knowledge that Nan Scott the Mother of Jin was free born.
Answer. I do not because she was older than myself.
Question by the same. Dont you know of your own knowledge that Jin Scott the daughter of Nan was born free.
Answer. I do.
Question by the same. Was it customary when you knew Jin Scott & for many years after for free born persons of colour to have any free papers.
Answer. No.

       Joseph Bailey

Sworn to & subscribed before me this 30th day of September 1831.
      Saml. Pleasants J.P. (Seal)

To Thomas T. Armstrong
Clerk of Stokes County North Carolina

Opened by the Clerk T.T. Armstrong

      Scott Vs Williams
      Jesse Scott Case

     State of North Carolina

To Samuel Pleasants Esquire

Stokes County

Esquires, Justice assigned to keep the Peace for Henrico County, and State of Virginia.

Know Ye, that we, reposeing special confidence in your fidelity and prudent circumspection, do authorise and empower you, that at such time and place as you shall appoint, you call and cause to come before you Joseph Bailey and him diligently examine on the Holy Evangelists of Almighty God, what he may know in and about a certain matter of controversy, now at issue in our Superior Court of Law, for the County of [Blank] wherein Jesse Scott by his next friend is Plaintiff, and Lewis Williams is Defendant, as well on the part of the Plaintiff as the Defendant; and such examination and deposition by you taken, you are to send, certified and enclosed, under your hands and seals, to the next Court to be held for said County, at the Court House in Germanton on the third Monday after the 4th Monday in September next; and this you shall in no wise omit.

Witness, Thomas T. Armstrong Clerk of our said Court, at office the 3rd Mon. after 4th Monday in March A.D. 1831 and in the fifty fifth year of our Independence.

Thos. T. Armstrong Clk.

Persuant to the annexed commission to me directed by the Honourable Superior Court of Stokes County North Carolina I caused Joseph Bailey to come before me Samuel Pleasants one of the Justices of the Peace for Henrico County State of Virginia at the House of said Joseph Bailey in said County on 30th day of September 1831 and Said Joseph Bailey being duly sworn to give evidence in the Suit now pending in Stokes Superior Court aforesaid wherein Jesse Scott by his next friend Mima Scott is Plaintiff and Lewis Williams is defendant to the several interrogatories to him proposed on his oath aforesaid deposeth and Saith as follows. Present Thomas Ladd Agent for Plaintiff & Wray Thomas for defendant.

Question by Plaintiff. Did you know a certain woman or girl in Henrico by the name of Jin Scott?
Answer. I did.
Question by same. What was her colour.
Answer. She was rather dark Complected.
Question by same. How old was Jin when you last saw her.

Stokes County

Answer. She was about twelve or thirteen years of age when I last saw her.
Question by same. How long has it been since you last saw Jin.
Answer. About Sixty odd years ago.
Question by same. Did you know Jins Mother - What was her name and was she or Jin claimed by any one as Slaves?
Answer. I knew her, her name was Nan Scott and neither her nor her daughter was ever claimed here as slaves.
Question by same. Were they taken and accepted as free persons in the community where they lived?
Answer. They were considered by every person who knew them to be free persons.
Question by same. Were they called Scott.
Answer. They were.
Question by same. Are John Burton and Thomas Ginnett dead? And did they die in Henrico.
Answer. I have no doubt of it from universal report.

Question by the Defendants Agent. Have you ever seen any writing purporting to give Jin Scotts Mother her freedom, or did you ever hear any one say he had ever seen such a writing?
Answer. I never have.
Question by same. All that you knew about the freedom of Jin Scotts Mother is that she passed in the neighborhood as a free woman of colour.
Answer. She passed as a free woman of colour.
Question by the same. You cant say that the Jin Scott whom you knew sixty odd years ago is the one mentioned in this Cause?
Answer. I cant say.

Question by the Plaintiffs agent. Dont you know of your own knowledge that Nan Scott the Mother of Jin was free born?
Answer I do not because she was older than myself.
Question by same. Dont you know of your own knowledge that Jin Scott daughter of Nan was born free?
Answer. I do.
Question by the same. Was it customary when you knew Jin Scott and for many years after for free born persons of colour to have any free papers?
Answer. No

Joseph Bailey

Stokes County

Sworn to & subscribed before me this 30th day of September 1831.
Saml. Pleasants J.P. (Seal)

To Thomas T. Armstrong Clerk of Stokes County.
Opened by the Clerk T.T. Armstrong

State of North Carolina
To J. Walsh esquire, Justice of the peace for the County of Wilkes & State of North Carolina Greeting.
We reposing especial Trust & Confidence in your integrity and ability do hereby authorise & empower you at such time and place as you shall appoint to cause to come before you Reuben Suttle and him Examine and his Deposition on oath to take in writing touching all such Matters & things as he may know concerning a Certain Matter of Controversy in our Superior Court of law pending wherein Malvina Scott is Plaintiff & Lewis Williams is Defendant and this deposition when by you so taken in fair Writing you will forward under your hands & Seals directed to the Judge of our next Superior Court of law to be held for the County of Stokes at the Court house in Germanton on the third Monday after the fourth Monday of September next to be read as evidence on behalf of the Plaintiff.
In Witness whereof I do hereto set my hand and Affix the seal of said Court at office the third Monday after the fourth Monday of March AD 1831.

Thos. T. Armstrong Clk.
North Carolina } on this 24th Day of June 1831
Wilkes County } I Caused Ruben Suttle to Come
before me J. Walsh at the house of Sd Suttle in obedience to the anexed Commition to me Directed by the Superior Court of Stokes the Sd Ruben Suttle being Duly Sworn to give Evidence in the Suit now pending in the Superior Cort of Stokes County and State of North Carolina where in Sally Scott is Plaintiff and Lewis Williams is Defendant Deposeth and Saith as follows

question by the plantiffs Agent

Stokes County

Did you know any thing of a dark woman named Jane Scot in the possession of William [?] Lewis
Answer I did
quet. by same
What do you know a bout the negros Jane & her children
Answer Said Lewis said he shoud have to send them to Cumberland that if he did not hee was afraid he should luse them I think the Names of the negros was those Jane Scot the mother & Sal Sillar Kisiah and Gabril as to any others I have forgot.
And further This Deponant Saith not.
Sworn to and Subscribed
This 24th June 1831   Reuben Suttle
Before Me J. Walsh JP

State of North Carolina

William N. Gileson Esquire
    One of the Justices assigned to keep the peace for Stokes County, and State of North Carolina.
    Know Ye, that we, reposing special confidence in your fidelity and prudent circumspection, do authorise and empower you, that at such time and place as you shall appoint, you shall call and cause to come before you Richard Sullivan and him diligently examine on the Holy Evangelists of Almighty God, what he may know in and about a certain matter of controversy, now at issue in our Superior Court of law for the County of Stokes wherein Jesse Scott by his next friend Jemima Scott is plaintiff, and Lewis Williams is defendant, as well on the part of the plaintiff as the defendant, and such examination and deposition by you taken, you are to send certified and enclosed, under your hands and seals, to the next court to be held for said county, at the Court House in Germanton on the third Monday After 4th Monday in Septemr. next: and this you shall in no wise omit.
    Witness Thomas T. Armstrong Clerk of our said Court, at Office the 2d day of April, Anno Domini 1831.
                                               Thos. T. Armstrong Clk.

Stokes County

Jemima Scott Vs. Lewis Williams & Others [1831]
Civil Action
Stokes County, NC

Jemima Scott Vs Lewis Williams
& others Vs Same
Notice deposition of Richd. Sullivan
Copy of the within left at the house of Maj: Jos. Williams, April 21st, A.D. 1831   R. Murchison
Mr. Joseph Williams
agent of Lewis Williams

     Sir take notice that on Saturday 23rd day of April instant I shall take the deposition of Richard Sullivan at the house of Thomas T. Armstrong in the town of Germanton Stokes County to be read in Evidence in the Suit now pending in Stokes Superior Court wherein Jemima Scott is Plaintiff and Lewis Williams is defendant Malvina Scott Plaintiff vs Lewis Williams defendant Jesse Scott by his next is Plaintiff and Lewis Williams is defendant and Sally Scott by her next friend is Plaintiff and Lewis Williams is defendant when and where you can attend and cross examine.

April 20th 1831   H.C. Jones
                                                                            Agent & atto. for Plff.

North Carolina   } Saturday April 23rd 1831
Stokes County   } Persuant to annexed Commission to me

directed I this day caused Richard Sullivan to come before me at the house of Thomas T. Armstrong in the town of Germanton in County and State aforesaid who first being duly Sworn to give Evidence in the Suit now pending in Stokes Superior Court of Jesse Scott by his next friend against Lewis Williams the said Richard Sullivan deposeth and Saith as follows (To wit)

Question by Plaintiffs agent
Are you acquainted with the Plaintiff Jesse Scott: If so, What is his pedigree and how do you know the Same?
Answer - In 1814-15 I knew a black woman called Mima Scott, at the house of Col: Joseph Williams in the County of Surry, and claimed by him as a Slave, She was the mother of Jane, who was in the possession of

Stokes County

Joseph Williams Jr. and who has since (I have been informed) obtained her freedom, Jin - Malvina - Polly - Sally - and Jesse who is the plaintiff in the Suit, those were called and recognized as the children of said Mima by Col: Jos. Williams and family white and black - I lived with Col: Williams as an overseer in the above years and also in 1818-19-20-21.

The aforesaid Mima was the Wife of John a Slave belonging to Col: Williams and was occasionally distinguished as John Mima - Col, Williams had another Mima who was extremely old so much so as to be beyond labouring - the Latter mentioned Mima had no children that I ever knew of - Mima Scott, from her appearance, when I left Col: Williams in 1821 - was not more than 40 to 45 years of age. Sworn to and Subscribed before me this 23rd April 1831 Richard Sillivan
W:N: Gibson J.P.

State of North Carolina

To William N. Gileson Esquire
One of the Justices assigned to keep the peace for Stokes County, and State of North Carolina

Know Ye, that we, reposing special confidence in your fidelity and prudent circumspection, do authorise and empower you, that at such time and place as you shall appoint, you call and cause to come before you Richard Sullivan and him diligently examine on the Holy Evangelists of Almighty God, what he may know in and about a certain matter of controversy, now at issue in our Superior Court of law for the County of Stokes wherein Sally Scott by her next friend Jemima Scott is plaintiff, and Lewis Williams is defendant, as well on the part of the plaintiff as the defendant, and such examination and deposition by you taken, you are to send certified and enclosed, under you hands and seals, to the next court to be held for said county, at the Court House in Germanton on the third Monday After 4th Monday in Septemr. next: and this you shall in no wise omit.

Witness Thomas T. Armstrong Clerk of our said Court, at Office, the 23d day of April, Anno Domoni 1831.
Tho. T. Armstrong Clk.

North Carolina } Saturday April 23rd 1831
Stokes County } Persuant to the annexed commission to me

Stokes County

directed I this day caused Richard Sullivan to come before me at the house of Thomas T. Armstrong in the town of Germanton in County and State aforesaid who first being duly Sworn to give Evidence in the Suit now pending in the Superior Court Stokes County of Sally Scott by her next friend against Lewis Williams the Said Richard Sullivan deposeth and Saith as follows towit.

Question by the Plaintiffs agent

Are you acquainted with Sally Scott if so what is her Pedigree and what are your opportunities of knowing the same

Answer - In 1814-15 I knew a black woman called Mima, sometimes distinguished as Mima Scott at the house of Col: Joseph Williams in the County of Surry, and claimed by him as a slave, She was the Mother of Sam (who has since I am informed, obtained his freedom), Jin, Malvina, ,Polly - Sally the plaintiff in the Suit and Jesse - who was called and recognized as the children of said Mima by Col. Williams and family white and black - I lived with Col Williams as an overseer in the above named year and also in 1818-19-20-21. The aforesaid Mima was the wife of John, a slave belonging to Col: Williams and was occasionally distinguished as John Mima - Col: Williams had also another Mima who was extremely old so much so as to be beyond labouring - Mima Scott did not appear to be more than 40 or 45 years of age when I left Col. Williams in 1821.

Richard Sullivan

Sworn to and Subscribed
before me 23rd. April 1831.   W:N: Gibson J.P.

State of North Carolina

To **[Blank]** Esquire, Justice of the Peace for **[Blank]** county, in the State of **[Blank]** Greeting:

We, reposing especial trust and confidence in your integrity and ability, do hereby authorise and empower you to cause to come before you, at such time and place as you shall appoint, Thomas Gennett & Joseph Bailey and them on oath examine, and their deposition in writing take, touching all such matters and things as they may know concerning a certain matter of controversy in our Court pending, wherein Mima Scott is plaintiff and Lewis Williams is defendant, and their deposition when by

Stokes County

you so taken in fair writing upon paper, you will forward under your hands and seals, directed to the Judge of our next Superior Court to be held for Stokes county, at the court house in Germanton on the 3rd Monday after the 4th Monday in March next, to be read as evidence in behalf of the Plaintiff.

In Testimony whereof, I Thomas T. Armstrong Clerk of our said Court, do hereunto subscribe my name and affix my seal of office, at Germanton the 3rd Monday after the 4th Monday in September A.D. 1830 Issued the 26th day of Decmr 1830.

Thos. T. Armstrong Clk.

State of Virginia } Persuant to a commission to
County of Henrico } me directed by the Honourable
Superior Court of Stokes County, I caused Joseph Bailey to come before me Samuel Pleasants one of the justices of the peace for Henrico County & State of Virginia at the house of said Joseph Bailey in the Said County of Henrico on the 8th day of April 1831. And the said Joseph Bailey being first duly Sworn to give evidence in the Suit pending in said Court wherein Mima Scott is Plaintiff and Lewis Williams is defendent to the several interrogatories to him propounded, and on his Corporal Oath declares as follows towit. Present Thomas Ladd agent for Plaintiff

Question by the plaintiffs agent. Did you know a woman or girl in Virginia by the name of Jin Scott?
Answer. I did.
Question by the same. How old was Jins mother when you knew her?
Answer. I knew her mother very well, but I have no distinct recollection of her age when she died.
Question by the same. What was Jins age?
Answer. She was about twelve or thirteen years of age when I last saw her.
Question by the same. What was her colour?
Answer. She was rather dark complected.
Question by the same. When did you last see her?
Answer. About sixty odd years ago.
Question by the same. Who was Jins mother, was she and her mother Nan ever to your knowledge claimed by any one as slaves?
Answer. Her name was Nan Scott and neither her nor her mother was ever claimed here by any person as slaves.
Question by the same. Were they taken and accepted as free persons?

Stokes County

Answer. They were considered by every person who knew them as free persons.
Question by the same. Were they called by the name of Scott?
Answer. They were.
Question by the same. Is John Burton dead?
Answer. I have no doubt of it from universal report.
        Joseph Bailey
Sworn to and Subscribed before me this 8th day of April 1831.
        Samuel Pleasants (J.P. (Seal)

Scott Vs Williams

State of Virginia   } Persuant to a commission to me
County of Henrico } directed by the Honourable Superior
Court of Stokes County, I caused Joseph Bailey to come before me Samuel Pleasants one of the justices of the Peace for Henrico County State of Virginia at the house of said Joseph Bailey in the said County of Henrico on the 8th day of April 1831 and the said Joseph Bailey being first duly sworn to give evidence, in the Suit pending in said Court, wherein Jesse Scott by his next friend Mima is Plaintiff and Lewis Williams is Defendant to the several interrogatories to him propounded on his corporal oath declareth as follows towit. Present Thomas Ladd agent for Plaintiff.

Question by the Plaintiffs Agent. Did you know a woman or girl in Virginia by the name of Jin Scott?
Answer. I did.
Question by the same. How old was Jins mother when you knew her?
Answer. I knew her Mother very well, but I have no distinct recollection of her age when she died.
Question by the same. What was Jins age?
Answer. She was about twelve or thirteen years of age when I last saw her.
Question by the same. What was her colour?
Answer. She was rather dark complected.
Question by the same. When did you last see her?
Answer. About sixty odd years ago.

Stokes County

Question by the same. Who was Jins Mother? Was she and her mother Nan ever to your knowledge claimed by any one as slaves?
Answer. Her name was Nan Scott and neither her nor her mother was ever claimed here by any person as slaves.
Question by the same. Were they taken and accepted as free persons?
Answer. They were considered by every person who knew them as free persons.
Question by the same. Were they called by the name of Scott?
Answer. They were.
Question by the same. Is John Burton dead?
Answer. I have no doubt of it from universal report.

        Joseph Bailey

Sworn to and Subscribed before me this 8th day of April 1831.

        Samuel Pleasants (J.P. (Seal)

    State of North Carolina

To [Blank] Esquire Justice of the Peace for [Blank] county, in the state of [Blank] Greeting:

 We, reposeing especial trust and confidence in your integrity and ability, do hereby authorise and empower you to cause to come before you, at such time and place as you shall appoint, Thomas Gennett & Joseph Bailey and them on oath examine, and their deposition in writing take, touching all such matters and things as they may know concerning a certain matter of controversy in our Superior Court pending, wherein Malvina Scott is plaintiff and Lewis Williams is defendant, and their deposition when by you so taken in fair writing upon paper, you will forward under your hands and seals, directed to the Judge of our next Superior Court to be held for Stokes County, at the court house in Germanton on the 3rd Monday after the 4th Monday in March next, to be read as evidence in behalf of the Plaintiff.

 In Testimony whereof, I Thomas T. Armstrong Clerk of said Court, do hereunto subscribe my name and affix my seal of office, at Germanton the 3rd Monday after the 4th Monday in September A.D. 1830 Issued 26th day of Decr. 1830.

        Tho. T. Armstrong Clk.

State of Virginia   } Persuant to a commission to me

Stokes County

County of Henrico } directed by the Honourable Superior Court of Stokes County, I caused Joseph Bailey to Come before me Samuel Pleasants one of the justices of the peace for Henrico County State of Virginia at the house of said Joseph Bailey in the said County of Henrico on the 8th day of April 1831. And the said Joseph Bailey being first duly sworn to give evidence in the Suit pending in the said Court, Wherein Malvina Scott [is Plaintiff] and Lewis Williams is Defendant, to the several interrogatories to him propounded on his corporal oath declareth as follows towit. present Thomas Ladd agent for Plaintiff.

Question by the Plaintiffs agent. Did you know a woman or girl in Virginia by the name of Jin Scott?
Answer. I did.
Question by the same. How old was Jins Mother when you knew her?
Answer. I knew her Mother very well, but have no recollection of her age when She died.
Question by the same. What was Jins age?
Answer. She was about twelve or thirteen years of age when I last saw her.
Question by the same. What was her colour?
Answer. She was rather dark complected.
Question by the same. When did you last see her?
Answer. About sixty odd years ago.
Question by the same. Who was Jins Mother, was she and her Mother Nan ever to your knowledge claimed by any one as slaves?
Answer. Her name was Nan Scott, and neither her nor her Mother was ever claimed here by any person as slaves.
Question by the same. Were they taken and accepted as free persons?
Answer. They were considered by every person who knew them as free persons.
Question by the same. Were they called by the name of Scott?
Answer. They were.
Question by the same. Is John Burton dead?
Answer. I have no doubt of it from universal report.

               Joseph Bailey

Sworn to and Subscribed before me this 8th day of April 1831.

               Samuel Pleasants JP (Seal)

Stokes County

We think a new trial should be granted, because the evidence of Davis as to the contents of the paper purporting to be a conveyance from Alley to Creson, ought not to have been admitted, as it had not been registered or recorded - as the subscribing Witness or the man who Davis believes to have been the subscribing Witness, has removed, but was not proven to be dead - as the hand writing of Creson was not proven, although the possession had not been consistent with the provisions of the deed.

Also, because the Judge rejected the deed from Lewis to Williams which was not offered as evidence of title, but as a circumstance to show that the negroes were treated as slaves, one of the subscribing witness were dead, the other had removed 25 years ago and we offered to prove the handwriting of Lewis, in this case the possession had run with the provisions of the deed. And because Jennetts deposition was read In the Ta[?] Because the court admitted the deposition of Bailey, which was taken in Virginia under a commission not under the Seal of the court.

North Carolina } Supr. Court of Law
Stokes County } Spring Term 1831

Jemima Scott vs Lewis Williams

Joseph Williams the agent of the Defendant & who is also concerned in interest in the above case maketh oath that William Davis & his two sons Ezra Davis & Jacob Davis are the securities for the prosecution of the above suit - that he is informed & so states the fact to be that both William Davis & his son Ezra Davis have sold their lands with a [?] to remove to the State of Tennessee or beyond the jurisdiction of this Court, & that Ezra has removed, that the third security Jacob Davis is the owner of a small & very poor piece of land & that the whole of the property of the said William Davis & Jacob Davis will be entirely unequal to the payment of the costs of this suit if the Pltff should fail. That the said William, Ezra & Jacob Davis are the securities in three other suits now pending in this Court against the said Defendant wherein, Malvina Scott, Sally Scott & Jesse Scott are the Plaintiffs - & that this affidavit extends to the whole of said suits.
Sworn to & Subscribed   J. Williams

Stokes County

in open Court   Thos. Armstrong Clk.

Surry County   } this Day Came Samuel Barnes Be fore me
James Adams
North Carolina   } one of the acting Justises of the Peace for sd.
October 12th, 1831   } County and sayeth upon oath that he thinks
that Jacob Davis is worth in property four hundred Dollars or upwards
Sworn to and Subscribed Before me
Test. Jas. Adams JP   Samuel Barnes

STATE OF NORTH CAROLINA

To William Gibson Esquire
    A Justice assigned to keep the Peace for Stokes County, and State of North Carolina.
    Know Ye, that we, reposing special confidence in your fidelity and prudent circumspection, do authorise and empower you, that at such time and place as you shall appoint, you call and cause to come before you Richard Sullivan and him diligently examine on the Holy Evangelists of Almighty God, what he may know in and about a certain matter of controversy, now at issue in our Superior Court of Law for the County of Stokes wherein Mima or Jesse or Malvina Scott is plaintiff, and Lewis Williams is defendant, as well on the part of the plaintiff as the defendant, and such examination and deposition by you taken, you are to send certified and enclosed, under your hands and seals, to the next court to be held for said county, at the Court House in Germanton on the 3rd Monday after the 4th Monday in September next: and this you shall in no wise omit.
Witness Thomas T. Armstrong Clerk of our said Court, at Office the 23d day of April, Anno Domini 1831
Thos. Armstrong Clk.

North Carolina   } Saturday April 23rd 1831
Stokes County   } Persuant to the annexed commission to me directed I this day caused Richard Sullivan to come before me at the house of Thomas T. Armstrong in the town of Germanton in County and State

Stokes County

aforesaid Who first being duly Sworn to give Evidence in the case now pending in the Superior Court of Stokes County of Mima Scott against Lewis Williams the said Richard Sullivan deposeth and Saith as follows to wit

Question by Plaintiffs agent - Are you acquainted with Mima Scott? if so Who is She and what is your knowledge founded on.

Answer - In 1814-15 I knew a black woman called Mima, and sometimes distinguished as Mima Scott, at the house of Col. Joseph Williams in the County of Surry, and claimed by him as a Slave. She was the mother of Sam, who was in the possession of of Joseph Williams Jr., and who has since, I have been informed obtained his freedom, Jim, Malvina - Polly - Sally and Jesse - have heard them called and recognized as the children of said Mima, by Col: Jos: Williams and family White and black, I lived with Col. Williams as an overseer in the above years and also in 1818-19-20-21- The aforesaid Mima was the Wife of John a Slave belonging to Col: Williams, and was occasionally distinguished as John's Mima. Col. Williams had also another Mima at the same time, who was extremely old so much so as to be beyond labouring, who had no children that I have ever heard of. Mima Scott, did not appear to be more than 40 or 45 years of age when I left Col: Williams in 1821.

Sworn to and Subscribed   Richard Sullivan
before me 23rd April 1831   W:N: Gibson J.P.

State of North Carolina
To William N. Gibson Esquire
    One of the Justices assigned to keep the Peace for Stokes County, and State of North Carolina.

    Know Ye, that we, reposing special confidence in your fidelity and prudent circumspection, do authorise and empower you, that at such time and place as you shall appoint, you call and cause to come before you Richard Sullivan and him diligently examine on the Holy Evangelists of Almighty God, what he may know in and about a certain matter of controversy, now at issue in our Superior Court of Law for the County of Stokes wherein Malvina Scott is plaintiff, and Lewis Williams is defendant, as well on the part of the plaintiff as the defendant, and such examination and deposition by you taken, you are to send certified and enclosed, under your hands and seals, to the next court to be held for said County, at the Court House in Germanton on the third Monday after 4

Stokes County

Monday in Septr. next: and this you shall in no wise omit. Witness Thomas T. Armstrong Clerk of our said Court, at Office the 23d day of April, Anno Domini 1831 Thos. Armstrong Clk.

North Carolina } Saturday April 23rd 1831
Stokes County } Persuant to the annexed commission to me directed I this day caused Richard Sullivan to come before me at the house of Thomas T. Armstrong in the town of Germanton in County and State aforesaid who first being duly Sworn to give Evidence in the Suit now pending in the Superior Court of Stokes County of Malvina Scott against Lewis Williams the said Richard Sullivan deposeth and Saith as follows (to wit)
Question by Plaintiffs agent - Are you acquainted with Malvina Scott? If so who is she &c.
Answer - In 1814-15 I knew a black woman, called Mima and sometimes Mima Scott, at the house of Col: Joseph Williams in the County of Surry, and claimed by him as a slave - She was the mother of Sam Who was in possession of Jos: Williams Jr., and has since (I am informed) obtained his freedom Jim - Malvina, Plaintiffs in this Suit, Polly - Sally and Jesse, who were called and recognized as the children of said Mima by Col: Williams & family White and black - I lived with Col: Williams in the above named years and also in 1818-19-20-21- The aforesaid Mima was the Wife of John a slave belonging to Col Williams and was occasionally distinguished as Johns Mima - Col: Williams had at the same time another Mima who was extremely old so much so as to be beyond labouring - Mima Scott was apparently not more than 40 or 45 years of age when I left Col: Williams in 1821.

Sworn to and Subscribed   Richard Sullivan
before me 23rd., April 1831
W:N: Gibson J.P.

[Editor's Note: This document is the front piece to a deposition sent under seal to the Clerk of Court of Stokes County.]

To The Clerk of the Superior
Court of Stokes County North Carolina

Stokes County

Scott   }
  vs   } Depos.
Williams   }

Opened by the Clerk
T.T. Armstrong

Mima Scott Vs Lewis Williams

Mima Scott
vs
Lewis Williams
Notice to take Deposition of
Reuben Suttle

I Delivered A Coppy of the within to Lewis Williams May the 11th AD 1831

                        Tho B Wright Shff
                        By E. Rutlege Ds.

Mr. Lewis Williams
      Take notice that on Friday 24th day of June next I shall attend at the dwelling house of Reuben Suttle Senr. in the County of Wilkes N.C. to take the depositions of said Reuben Suttle & others to be read as Evidence in a certain Suits now pending in the Superior Court of Stokes County Viz Jemima Scott Vs. yourself Malvina Scott Vs. Same Jesse Scott by his next friend Vs. Same & Sally Scott by her next friend Vs. Same.
May 10th 1831   H.C. Jones
                                   Atto. for plffs

Scotts Vs. Williams
Notice to take Depositions

I Delivered A Coppy of the within to Lewis Williams May the 11th AD 1831.

Stokes County

Tho B Wright   Shff
By E. Rutlege Ds.

Mr. Lewis Williams
    Take notice that the depositions of Joseph Bailey will be taken at his house in the County of Henrico State of Virginia on Thursday 16th of June next and if not on that day then on the next at same place and if not then it will be taken there on Saturday 18th of Same month to be read as Evidence in the Suits now pending in Stokes Superior Court to wit Jemima Scott Vs yourself Malvina Scott Vs same Jesse Scott by his next friend Vs same & Sally Scott by her next friend Vs same.
                                H.C. Jones
May 11th, 1831   Atto for Plffs.

State of North Carolina
To   J. Walsh Esquires Justices of the Peace
for the County of Wilkes & State of North Carolina Greeting.
    We reposing special trust & Confidence in your integrity & ability do hereby authorise and empower you to Cause to Come before you at such time and place as you shall appoint: Reuben Suttle and him on oath examine and his deposition in writing take touching all such matters & things as he may know concerning a Matter of Controversy in our Superior Court of law pending wherein Jemima Scott is Plaintiff and Lewis Williams is Defendant And Deposition when so taken by you in fair writing you will forward under your hands & Seals directed to the Judge of our Next Superior Court of law to be held for the County of Stokes at the Court house in Germanton on the third Monday after the fourth Monday of September next, to be read as evidence on behalf of the Plaintiff In Witness whereof I Thomas T Armstrong Clerk of our said Court do hereto set my hand and afix the seal of said Court at office the third Monday after the fourth Monday of March Ad 1831.
                        Tho. T. Armstrong

North Carolina } on this 24th Day of June 1831
Wilks County   } I Caused Reuben Suttle to Come
before me John Walsh at the house of Sd. Suttle in obedience to the anexed Commition to me directed by the Superior Court of Stokes the Sd.

Stokes County

Reuben Suttle being Duly Sworn to give Evidence in the Suit now pending in the Superior Court of Stokes County and State of North Carolina where in Jemima Scott is plaintiff and Lewis Williams is Defendant Deposeth and Saith as follows--
Did you know any thing of a dark woman Named Jane Scot in the posesion of William Terel Louis
Answer I did
que. What do you know about them negros Jane & her children
A Said Louis Said hee shood have to send them to cumberland That if he did not he was afraid hee should lose them I think The Names of the negros were these Jane Scot the mother and Sal & Sillar and Kiseah & Gabriel as to any others I have forgot
and further This Deponent Saith not
Sworn to and Subscribd.   Reuben Suttle
Before Me this 24th June 1831
J. Walsh JP

North Carolina   }   on this 24th Day of June 1831
Wilks County   }   I Cause Reuben Suttle to Come
before me John Walsh at the house of Sd. Suttle in obedience to the anexed Commition to me Directed by the Superior Court of Stokes the Sd. Reuben Suttle being Duly Sworn to give Evidence in the Suit now pending in the Superior Court of Stokes County and State of North Carolina where in Malvina Scott is plaintiff and Lewis Williams is Defendant Deposeth and Saith as follows,
question by the plantiffs agent
Did you know any thing of a dark woman Namd. Jane Scott in posesion of William Terel Lewis
Answer I did
qu. What do you know about them negroes Jane Scot and Her children
Answer Said Lewis Said hee should have to send them to Cumberland that if hee did not hee was afraid hee should loose them I think the names of the negroes were These Jane Scot the mother & sal & sillar kisiah and gabriel as to any others I have forgot And further this Deponant Saith not
Sworn to and subscribed   Reuben Suttle
Before Me This 24th June 1831
J. Walsh JP

Stokes County

State of North Carolina
    To Jn. Walsh Esquire Justice of the Peace for the County of Wilkes and State of North Carolina Greeting
    We reposing especial trust and Confidence in your integrity and ability do hereby empower you at such time and place as you shall appoint to Cause to Come before you Reuben Suttle and him examine on oath and his deposition on oath to take in writing touching all such matters as he may know concerning a certain Matter of Controversy now pending in our Superior Court of Law Wherein Jesse Scott by his next friend is Plaintiff and Lewis Williams is defendant and his deposition when by you taken you will forward under your hands and Seals directed to our Superior Court to be held for the County of Stokes at the Court house in Germanton on the third Monday after the fourth Monday in September next AD 1831 to be read as Evidence in behalf of the Plaintiff. In Witness whereof I do hereto set my hand & Affix the seal of said Court at Office the third Monday after the fourth Monday of **[Blank]** AD 1831
        Tho T Armstrong Clk

North Carolina } on this 24th Day of June 1831
Wilks County } I Cause Reuben Suttle
to Come before me Jn. Walsh at the house of Sd. Suttle in obediance to the anexed Commition to me directed by the Superior Court of Stokes the Sd. Reuben Suttle being Duly Sworn to give Evidence in the Suit now pending in the Superior Court of Stokes County and State of North Carolina wherein Jesse Scott is plantiff and Lewis Williams is Defendant Deposeth and Saith as follows
question by the plantiffs Agent
Did you know any thing of a dark woman Namd. Jane Scot in the posesion of William Terel louis
Answer I did
qu. What do you know about them negroes Jane Scot and her children.
Answer Said Louis said hee should have to send them to cumberland that if hee did not hee was afraid he should loose them I think the Names of the the negroes are these Jane Scot the mother & sal & sillar kisiah & gabriel as to any others I have forgot And further this Deponant saith not
Sworn to & subscribd.   Reuben Suttle
this 24th June 1831

Stokes County

Jn. Walsh   JP

State of North Carolina
To Samuel Pleasants Esq

  Esquires, Justices assigned to keep the Peace for Henrico County, and State of Virginia.
  Know Ye, that we, reposing special confidence in your fidelity and prudent circumspection, do authorise and empower you, that at such time and place as you shall appoint, you call and cause to come before you Joseph Bailey and him diligently examine on the Holy Evangelists of Almighty God, what he may know in and about a certain matter of controversy, now at issue in our Superior Court of Law, for the County of Stokes wherein Mima or Jemima Scott is Plaintiff, and Lewis Williams is Defendant, as well on the part of the Plaintiff as the Defendant; and such examination and deposition by you taken, you are to send, certified and enclosed, under your hands and seals, to the next Court to be held for said County, at the Court House in Germanton on the third Monday after 4th Monday in September next; and this you shall in no wise omit.
  Witness, Thomas T. Armstrong Clerk of our said Court, at Office the third Monday after 4th Monday in March A.D. 1831 and in the fifty fifth year of our Independence.
       Tho T Armstrong Clk.

Scott (Mima) vs Williams
Opened by the Clerk T.T. Armstrong

To Thomas T. Armstrong Clerk of Stokes County North Carolina

Persuant to the annexed commission to me directed by the Honourable Superior Court of Stokes County North Carolina I caused Joseph Bailey to come before me Samuel Pleasants One of the Justices of the Peace for Henrico State of Virginia at the house of said Bailey in Said County of Henrico on Friday 30th day of September AD 1831 and the said Joseph Bailey being duly Sworn to give evidence in the Suit pending in Said Superior Court of Stokes Wherein Mima or Jemima Scott is plaintiff and Lewis Williams is defendant to the Several interrogatories to him

Stokes County

proposed on his oath aforesaid declareth and Saith as follows to wit. Present Thomas Ladd agent for Plaintiff & Wray Thomas for Defendant.
Question by Plaintiff Did you know a woman or girl in this county by the name of Jin Scott
Answer I did
Question by same How old was Jin when you last saw her.
Answer She was twelve or thirteen years of age when I last saw her.
Question by Same What was her colour
Answer She was rather dark complected.
Question by Same When did you last see Jin
Answer About sixty odd years ago.
Question by Same Did you know Jins Mother if so what was her name and was she or Jin claimed as a Slave by any one.
Answer I knew her, her name was Nan Scott and neither her nor her daughter was ever claimed here as slaves.
Question by Same Were they taken and accepted by the community as free persons?
Answer They were considered by every person who knew them to be free persons.
Question by Same Were they called Scott
Answer They were
Question by Same Are John Burton & Thomas Gennett generally reported to be dead? & did they die in Henrico.
Answer I have no doubt of it from universal report

Question by defendants agent Have you ever seen any writing purporting to give Jin Scotts Mother her freedom or did you ever hear any one say that he had seen such writing?
Answer I never have
Question by Same All that you knew about the freedom of Jin Scotts Mother is that she passed in the neighborhood as a free Woman of Colour?
Answer She passed as a free woman of colour.
Question by Same You cant say that the Jin Scott who you knew sixty odd years ago is the one mentioned in this Cause?
Answer I cant say.
Question by the Plaintiffs agent Dont you know of your own knowledge that Nan Scott the Mother Jin was free born?
Answer I do not because she was older than myself

Stokes County

Question by Same Dont you know of your own that Jin Scott the daughter of Nan was born free.
Answer I do.
Question by the Same Was it customary when you knew Jin Scott and for many years after for free born Persons of Colour to have any free papers.
Answer No.

Joseph Bailey

Sworn to & Subscribed before Me this 30th day of September 1831.

Saml. Pleasants JP (S)

The Scotts Vs Lewis Williams
Notice
Came to hand August the 10th 1831
Tho B Wright Shff
By E. Rutlege Ds.

I delivered a Coppy of the within to Lewis Williams August 10th 1831

Tho B Wright Shff
By E. Rutlege Ds.

Mr. Lewis Williams

Take notice that I shall attend at the house of Joseph Bailey in the County of Henrico State of Virgia. on Thursday the 29th day of September next to take the depositions of Joseph Bailey and others to be read in evidence in the Several Suits now pending in the Superior Court of Stokes County of Jemima Scott against you Malvina Scott vs you Jesse Scott by his next friend against you and Sally Scott by her next friend against you and if the deposition is not taken I shall attend at the Same place on the next day - and if not then taken on the next day after that when and where you can attend and cross examine if you think proper.

August 10th 1831   H.C. Jones
Atto. for plffs

Scott Vs Williams
Afft.

Stokes County

North Carolina } Supr. Court of Law
Stokes County } Spring Term 1832
Jemima Scott Vs Lewis Williams

    Joseph Williams maketh oath, that the Deft claims title to the Pltff. thro' the will of his father the late Col. Joseph Williams as one of the Executors thereof, & that this affiant is also one of the Exrs. that he has been from the commencement of the suit, the agent by whom the defence has been managed on the part of the Defendant - He further states that since the tryal of this suit, he has come to the knowledge of evidence, by which he expects & believes he shall be able to show that the Jane Scott spoken of by the witnesses as formerly living in Henrico County in Virginia was a Slave & that her mother Nan was also a Slave - that the information was given to him since the tryal by Mr. Irby Smith, who lives in the County of Person in this State, & who is in attendance at this Court as a witness in another case - & that this is as he believes the first Court that Mr. Smith has attended as a witness & that he did not know of the existence of the facts communicated by him untill since the tryal of the cause - nor does he believe the Dft. now knows him He further states that other such have been heretofore bro't by other members of Jane Scotts descendants to recover their freedom, against this affiant to the persons claiming them and he states that he has on some of the different tryals preceeding this been instructed by his counsel that it was not necessary to have deed from W.T. Louis to his father proved & registered - that he believes he can prove the hand writing of the subscribing witnesses He further states that on the tryal of the suit of Mima Scott against Badgett - the objection was made to the reading of one of the deeds of Dft upon the same ground as in this case and that the Court over ruled the objection & the deed was read.

Joseph Williams maketh oath that the matters of fact Set forth in this affidavit as of his own knowledge are true & those set forth as not of his own knowledge he believes to be true
Sworn to & subscribed   Jo Williams
this **[Blank]** day of April 1832
Tho T Armstrong Clk

Stokes County

North Carolina Stokes County

Jemima Scott   }
    vs   } Superior Court April Term 1832
Lewis Williams }

      Irby Smith maketh oath that the information given to Mr. Joseph Williams relative to the above case was that about the year 1819 or 1820 this affiant was present at a trial in the County Court of Halifax Va between some negroes and other persons which trial was for the purpose of establishing the freedom of said negroes & that said negroes claimed their freedom through a woman called Free Nan who lived in Henrico Va as appeared from the testimony and further that a negro man now about seventy years old who was one of the Plaintiffs in their Suits informed Affiant that he was the youngest of Nan's Children & that he had a Sister named Jin who was the oldest of said Children and who was carried away back   This Affiant further informed said Williams that these Suits were determined against the Plaintiffs   Affiant does not remember the particulars of the testimony given in said case nor does he remember that any of said negroes or said Woman Nan was called by the name of Scott.

                                        Irby Smith

Sworn to & subscribed
in open Court
Tho. T. Armstrong Clk

Stokes County North Carolina

Jemima Scott   } Superior Court April Term 1832
    Vs   }
Lewis Williams } Hamilton C Jones Maketh oath that he has been concerned in the management of the Suits for the descendants of Nan Scott and Jin Scott as agent & Attorney that as far back as ten years ago as he believes the depositions of Joseph Bailey and two others were taken in the County of Henrico Va in the very neighborhood where these negroes were said to have lived and that Joseph Williams Junr. has always taken a very deep interest in taking said depositions - that Plaintiffs by agents have more than six different times attended to take depositions since the first were taken there, and that the agents of said Williams and others

Stokes County

have most commonly attended to cross examine. He further Swears that Joseph Williams Junr. who has had the active management of almost all of these Suits, has had depositions taken in said County several times for the avowed purpose of proving said Nan and Jenny to be Slaves, and of discrediting the testimony of Joseph Bailey Thomas Gennett and John Burton, and as far as this affiant can Judge has always failed in such proof entirely. He believes that the most industrious means have been used to procure the testimony in Henrico which he says he has lately heard of, without success.
H.C. Jones
Sworn to & subscribed
in open Court
Tho T Armstrong

Notice from Lewis Williams to H.C. Jones
Fall Term 1832
Executed by Delivering a Copy to H.C. Jones
August 1832
F Slater

Mr. Hamilton C Jones
  Take notice that I shall attend on Monday the 3rd day of September next at the Store house of Samuel Watkins in the Town of Milton in the County of Caswell North Carolina and shall then and there in the hours of 10 Oclock in the morning and 2 Oclock in the evening, proceed to take the deposition of George Claughton and others to be read in evidence in the Suit now pending in Stokes Superior Court of Law, wherein Jemima Scott is plaintiff and myself defendant, when and where you may attend and cross examine if you think proper. Also take notice that I shall attend at the Court House in Person County North Carolina on Wednesday the 5th of September next and between the hours of 10 Oclock in the morning and 2 Oclock in the evening shall proceed to take the deposition of Thomas Allen and others to be read in evidence in the aforesaid Suit wherein Jemima Scott is plaintiff and myself defendant when and where you may attend and cross examine if you think proper. Also take further notice that I shall attend on Friday the 28th of September next at the dwelling house of Thomas Crawley in Halifax County Virginia and between the hours of 10 Oclock in the morning and

Stokes County

2 Oclock in the evening shall proceed to take the deposition of said Thomas Crawley and others to be read in evidence in the aforesaid Suit now pending in Stokes Superior Court of Law wherein Jemima Scott is plaintiff and myself defendant, where and when you may attend and cross examine if you think proper.

Lewis Williams

Surry County }
August 8th 1832 }

North Carolina } Supr. Court of Law
Stokes County } Fall Term 1833
Jemima Scott vs Lewis Williams
M. Scott vs Same
J. Scott vs Same
S. Scott vs Same

Joseph Williams the agent of the Defendant in the above cases maketh oath that the testimony of Richard Wilbourne is as he advised material & necessary for the Deft. that by said witness he expects to prove that the testimony of Thos. Settle whose deposition is filed in these cases on behalf of the Pltffs. is false - that he was not untill last night, upon conversing with his counsel, advised that it was necessary to have him summoned he further states that heknew before last court what the said Welbourne would prove but was induced not to summon him from a belief that the testimony of Settle referred to a conversation of William T. Lewis made subsequent to the sale of the negroe Jemima, the Pltff in the first action and mother of the others, to the Dfts. Testator & that therefore it would not be admitted in evidence. He further swears that the Testimony of certain other witnesses living in and about Richmond in Virginia is material & necessary for the Deft. - that by said witnesses he expects to prove that Joseph Bailey a witness for the Pltffs. is a man of such infamy of character as to be unworthy of belief - that the Deft. gave to Hamilton C. Jones the Atty. of the Pltffs. notice to take the depositions of said witnesses - in the City of Richmond in due time & that he wrote to a friend to wit Wray Thomas a lawyer of that place to attend to the taking of the deposition & sent on to him at the same time a series of interrogatories drawn up by one of his counsel, to proposition to said witnesses & that he has since learnt that the said Thomas was at the time the depositions were

Stokes County

to be taken absent in the State of Ohio - that Dft. was at the Springs in Virginia during the summer on acct. of his health from which he did not return untill within ten days past. That owing to the absence of the said Wray Thomas he presumes the depositions were not taken as they had not been sent on & deponent does not believe the cases can be safely tried without them. He states further that he believes that John Kerr was one of the witnesses whose deposition was to be taken in Virginia at Richmond but is not certain as he has no copy of the notice served on Mr. Jones - & [?] application to him for a sight of the notice - he is informed by him that he has it not - he knows that Mr. Kerr is one of the witnesses relied on by Deft.

Sworn to & subscribed   Jo Williams
in open Court
Tho. T. Armstrong Clk.

Virginia, To Wit:

    I, John Floyd Governor of the State afiresaid, do hereby certify, and make known unto ALL WHOM IT MAY CONCERN, that William W. Mcrery whose name is so subscribed to a Certificate subjoined to the annexed documents was at the time of subscribing the same, a Notary Public for the City of Richmond duly commissioned and qualified according to Law, and to all his Official Acts as such full faith, credit and authority, are had and ought to be given.

    IN TESTIMONY WHEREOF, I have subscribed my name, and caused the Great Seal of the State to be affixed hereunto. Done at the City of Richmond, the twenty first day of September in the year of our Lord one thousand eight hundred and thirty three and of the Commonwealth the fifty eighth

By The Governor
Wm H Richardson   }
Keeper of the Seal   }   John Floyd

                Jemima Scott Vs Lewis Williams
                                      &c
            Copy of Notice to take depositions

Mr. H.C. Jones

Stokes County

I shall at the court house of the County, in Richmond, in the County of Henrico State of Virginia, on the 18th, 19th and 20th days of September take the Depositions of John Kerr and others to be read as evidence at the trial of the case now pending in the Superior Court of Law and equity for the County of Stokes viz. Jemima Scott (so called) plaintf. vs. Lewis Williams, Dft., Malvina Scott (so called) vs. Same, Mary Scott (so called) by her next friend vs. Same and Jesse Scott (so called) by his next friend vs. Same, - you can attend as the agent of the plaintiffs and cross examine if you see proper.

July 12th, 1833   Lewis L. Williams

Commonwealth of Virginia
City of Richmond, to wit:

  The foregoing and within depositions of John Pearce and John Talman were taken, sworn and subscribed to, before me, the undersigned, a Notary Public, duly commissioned and qualified in and for the City aforesaid.

In testimony whereof, I have hereunto set my hand and affixed my Notarial Seal of Office, this twentieth day of September, in the Year One thousand eight hundred and thirty three.
W.W. McCreery Not: Pub:

Jemima Scott v. Williams	}
Malvina Scott v. Same	}
Mary Scott v. Same	} Depositions
Jesse Scott v. Same	}

The Depositions of John Pearce and John Talman taken, according to law, before William W. McCreery a Notary Public for the City of Richmond in the State of Virginia, on the twentieth day of September in the year 1833, at the Court House of the County of Henrico, in said City, in pursuance of the Copy of a Notice, hereto annexed, to be read in evidence in the suits of Jemima Scott vs: Lewis Williams, Malvina Scott vs: the same, Mary Scott, by her next friend, vs: the same, and Jesse Scott, by his next friend, vs: the same, now pending in the Superior Court of law & Equity for the County of Stokes, in the State of North Carolina.

Stokes County

John Pearce, being first duly sworn on the Holy Evangelists, deposeth and saith,

Question by Defendant - Were you well acquainted with Joseph Bayley?
Answer - I was.
Question by same - Did he not associate upon terms of equality with negroes?
Answer - There was a Mulatto woman named Edie Scott, who lived on his land, and she had several children, which he owned as his and left his estate to them, by Will, which is on Record.
Question by same - What was his age in 1823?
Answer - Seventy years old.
Question by same - Was he, or, was henot as capable of giving evidence at that time, as he ever was?
Answer - I should think that his memory had failed him on account of his age.
Question by same - Were his affections toward his relations of a very strong nature?
Answer - He did not treat his relations with affection.
Question by same - In what manner did he live as regards cleanliness?
Answer - I cannot say as to his cleanliness, He lived with a Mulatto woman and her children - and very few respectable persons visited him.
And further this deponent saith not.
                                        John Pearce

John Talman being first duly sworn on the Holy Evangelists deposeth and saith

By the Defendant - State what you know about Joseph Bayley's association with Edie Scott & his manner of living?
Answer - I had occasion to go to his house. I saw there a mulatto woman who was said to be his kept mistress, and several children, also mulattoes, said to be his.
Question by Same - Was he visited by his neighbours? and in what estimation Was he held by them?
Answer - I do not think that he was visited by his neighbours, except on business - My own family would not have visited him.
And further this deponent saith not

Stokes County

John Talman

Memorandum for the Clerk in making up the cases of
The Scotts vs. Williams

Mem for Mr. Armstrong

The deed Signed by James Ally And Jane Scott which you are to copy as part of Mimas Case you will find attached to the Depositions of Isaiah Coe and Saml. L. Davis among your court papers - In this Memorandum you will find the other copies which you are to transcribe. I want you to take good care of these - And Send me the records by Mr. Boyden to Surry County Court in November (2nd Monday).

Bailey has given two Depositions; the One to be sent up is on the outside of the court file Marked A.

H.C. Jones

In the cases of Sally & Jesse Scott you need not make up any case nor copy any papers.

Scott }
vs } Depos.
Williams }

To the Clerk of Stokes Superior Court
Opened by the Clerk
T T Armstrong

State of North Carolina }
Stokes County }

Persuant to a commission to us directed by the Superior Court of Stokes County We,

Proceeded at the house of Reuben Golding in Germanton to take the depositions of Isaiah Coe and Samuel L. Davis to be read in Evidence in the Suit of Jemima Scott vs Lewis Williams on this the 15th day of October 1833 present H.C. Jones agent for the Plaintiff and Joseph Williams agent for the defendant.

Stokes County

State of North Carolina
To William C. Cole and Peter Transue
Esquires, Justices assigned to keep the Peace for County, and State of North Carolina.

Know Ye, that we, reposing special confidence in your fidelity and prudent circumspection, do authorise and empower you, or any of you, that at such time and place as you shall appoint, you call and cause to come before you Isaiah Coe & Samuel L. Davis and them diligently examine on the Holy Evangelist of Almighty God, what they may know in and about a certain matter of controversy, now at issue at our Superior Court of Law, for the county of Stokes wherein Jemima Scott is Plaintiff, and Lewis Williams is Defendant, as well on the part of the Plaintiff as the Defendant; and such examination and deposition by you taken, you are to send, certified and enclosed, under your hand and seals, to the next Court to be held for said County, at the Court House in Germanton on the third Monday after the 4th Monday in March next; and this you shall in no wise omit.

Witness, Thomas T Armstrong Clerk of our said Court, at office the third Monday after the fourth Monday of September A.D. 1833 and in the fifty 8 year of our Independence.

Tho T Armstrong

State of North Carolina
Stokes County

Pursuant to the annexed comission to us directed and under the rule of court at next term we proceeded on Tuesday the 15 of October 1833 at the house of Reuben Golding in the town of Germanton Stokes Co. N.C. to take the depositions of Isaiah Coe and Samuel L Davis to be read in evidence in the suit now pending in the Superior Court of Stokes County wherein Jemima Scott is Pltf and Lewis Williams is defendant - H.C. Jones agent for the Plaintiff and Joseph Williams agent for the defendant being present And the said Isaiah Coe being duly sworn deposeth and Saith as follows to wit.

Isaiah Coe being first examined deposeth and saith, that he first knew Jane Scott sixty four or five years ago or there abouts at Abraham Cresons in Rowan County now the County of Surry, that he understood from the said Abraham Creson that the said Jane Scott came into his

Stokes County

possession from a man by the name of Ally, that said Jane Scott was at that time pregnant & thinks that she was young to be in that condition, that this woman was commonly in the family of said Creson called Jane Scott or free Jin on account of there being two others by the name of Jane in the same family, that he visited Abraham Creson on a certain occasion & heard him complain that the children of said Jane Scott had been taken out of his possession & bound out by the County Court of Surry, that had the Court have bound them to him for the same length of time where they would have been treated equally as well or allowed him some compensation in money for raising them he would have been perfectly satisfied, that said Creson went on to observe that several of these children at that time were able to earn their victuals & clothes, that neither in his conversation nor in no other conversation did he ever hear the said Creson complain of the said Jane Scotts being taken away by the Court.

   The witness being asked as to the children of Jane Scott says that while she lived with Abraham Creson she had several children, the first was a bright mulatto called Sal Ally & generally called in the family the child of James Ally & generally called in the family the child of James Ally, the name of the second he thinks was Kiziah, the name of another was Jemima, the name of another was Karanhapuc, that he understood from Abraham Creson that Jemima was bound to Joseph Williams (Col.)

Question by the Defendants agent? Did you ever hear Abraham Creson say whether the said Jane Scott was a free woman or not

Ans. I can not say certainly whether I ever heard Creson say so, but I have frequently heard his family say so.

Question by the Defendants agent - Did you ever hear any of the family say that she was free except David Enyart

Ans. I did hear several of the Enyart family say so besides David, also several of the Wainscott family who were Cresons sisters children These Enyarts were Cresons step children & lived with him.

Question by the Defendants agent - How old were you when you first saw Jane Scott in the possession of Abraham Creson

Ans. I was about seven eight or nine years old, at which time I was in the habit of going to mill & to school.

Question by the Defendants agent - Was not Abraham Creson what was called a tory.

Ans. He was

Question by the Defendants agent - Was not John Hudspeth called a warm & zealous whig.

Stokes County

Ans. He was.
Question by the Plffs agent - Were you a near neighbour to said Creson & were you intimate with his family
Ans. Yes, I was. I lived in a mile & a half of them & was very intimate with them.
Question by Plffs agent Do you or do you not **[Faded]** that you have heard Jane Scott called free Jin in the presence of Abm. Creson?
Ans. I do believe that I have often.
Sworn to & subscribed this 15th   Isaiah Coe
day of Octr. 1833 before us at the
time & place above stated
Jn C Cole J.P.
P. Transu J.P.

Samuel L. Davis being then examined deposeth & sayeth
    That he found the annexed paper writing among the papers of Joshua & Abraham Creson, that he was one of the administrators of Joshua Creson & that George Creson was the other administrator of Joshua Creson, that the said Joshua Creson was the son & Executor of the said Abraham Creson that this deponent took possession of the papers of the said Joshua & Abraham Creson & found the annexed paper among them that since the said paper came into his possession he has attached it to another paper with thread as it now appears & that the writing has in no respect been altered since it came into his possession.
Sworn to & subscribed   Saml L Davis
the day & place above stated
W.C. Cole J.P.
P. Transu J.P.

             Jemima Scott & others vs Lewis Williams
                       Copy of notice
                       Octr. 18th, 1833

I handed this paper to Hamilton C. Jones, and he Read the contents of it in my presence.
    S. Stone Shff.

Stokes County

Mr H C Jones

    I shall at the Court House of the County of Henrico in the City of Richmond State of Virginia on the 18th of November next, take the depositions of John Kerr and others to be read in evidence at the trial of the causes now pending in the Superior Court of Law and Equity for the County of Stokes towit Jemima Scott (so called) plaintiff vs Lewis Williams Defendant; Melvina Scott (so called) vs the same; Sally Scott (so called) by her next friend vs the same; and Jesse Scott (so called) by his next friend vs the same You will also further take notice that if not completed on that day; the business of taking the depositions as above stated will be continued at the same place day to day untill it is completed - You can attend as the agent of the plaintiffs and cross examine if you think proper.

Surry County   }   Lewis Williams
Octo. 17th, 1833

North Carolina } Supr. Court of Law
Stokes County   } Spring Term 1834

Jemima Scott vs Lewis Williams
M. Scott   vs Same
S. Scott   vs Same
J. Scott   vs Same

    Joseph Williams the agent of the Defendant in the above cases maketh oath that Charles Steelman is a material necessary witness for Deft. in the above case, that he has been subponaed & is absent without his consent or that of Deft. as he believes that by said witness he expects to prove that he was the son in law of Creson & that he knew a negro woman by the name of Jane while in the possession of Creson & who it is alleged by Pltffs. was the mother of the first & the grandmother of the others - that said Jane was a black woman - that he knew her for several years, while so in Cresons possession who during the whole of the time claimed & used her as a slave - that he always understood that Creson had purchased her for a valuable consideration from one Ally & that the reason why Ally sold her was that it was reported that he kept her & that his wife was jealous of her & that said witness was the son in law of

Stokes County

Creson & [?] never heard in the family or otherwise any rumors or report that Jane was free untill after Hudspeth Commenced his proceedings in the County Court of Surry & further that Creson sold Jane to W.T. Lewis
Sworn to & Subscribed in open Court   Jo Williams
April 16th 1834
T T Armstrong Clk

Jemima Scott & others
vs
Lewis Williams
Deposition

Came to hand September the 6th, 1834
Thos. Wright shff.
By E. Rutledge Ds
I delivered a Coppy of the within to Hamilton C Jones September the 6th 1834
Tho. B. Wright shff
By E. Rutledge DS.

Hamilton C Jones Esq.
    You are hereby notified to produce before the Next Superior Court of Law of Stokes County the Deposition of Isaiah Coe taken in the Suit Jime & Abraham Badgett In the Superior Court of Iredell County to be read in evidence in the Suits pending in the Superior Court of Law in Stokes County in which Jemima Scott Melvina Scott & the others severally are Plaintiffs & Lewis Williams is Defendant or I shall offer evidence of its contents.
September 6, 1834   Lewis Williams
                                              By Jo Williams agt.

The Scotts vs Lewis Williams
Agreemant of counsel to go to Supreme Court

    It is agreed between us that transcripts go up in the case of Jemima Scott vs Lewis Williams.

Stokes County

Also in the case of Malvina Scott vs Lewis Williams (record in the last mentioned case be rec.) And that the cases of Jesse Scott and Sally Scott (in the Supreme Court as record in the cases of) vs the same. It is agreed that one set of the copies of the papers ordered in the statement of the Judge to form a part of the case be made out & read in the Supreme Court in the others.

       H.C. Jones for Plff
       F. Nash for Dt.

Jemima Scott vs Lewis Williams
  This was on action against the Defendant for assault Battery & imprisonment, to which the Defendant pleaded that the Pltf was a slave, on which issue was joined, on the trial the case was treated & so considered by the parties as a Suit revived which had been brought against Joseph Williams the Defendants testator, & revived against the Defendt. as his Executor, & under that apprehension had been in all respects managed & treated, till after the verdict of the Jury & the motion for a new trial. The motion for a new trial was on the grounds, of excessive damages & misdirection of the Court in its instructions to the Jury as to the damages & the admission of improper evidence on the part of the Plaintiff. The Pltf offered & was permitted to give in evidence the order of the County Court of Surry in the year 1779 binding the Plaintiff to Joseph Williams, the Father & testator of the defendant & also the Indenture Signed by the Chairman of the Court & the Said Joseph Williams in which the Plaintiff is recognized as Jemima Scott a free person & bound until she arrives at the age of eighteen. It appeared also that Joseph Williams was at that time Clerk of Surry Court. The record of the order of Surry Court, also set forth that the Mother of the Plaintiff, & other children besides the Pltff had been brought before the Court on a habeas Corpus directed to the Sheriff whilst they were declared as Slaves Copies of which record & Indenture form part of this case. The Plaintiff also gave in evidence the deposition of Joseph Bailey a Copy of which forms part of this Case. The Pltf also gave evidence to prove that the present Pltf was the same person bound to Joseph Williams by the indenture before stated. The Defendant then gave in evidence a record of the Superior Court of Salisbury district of proceedings at the Instance of Abram Creson complaining of error in the proceedings under the habeas Corpus, & the Judgment of the Court thereon Copy of which form part of

Stokes County

the case The Plaintiff then gave in evidence a deed from James Alley & Jane Scott the mother of the plaintiff to the said Abram Creson dated in Jany 1768 a Copy of which forms also part of this Case. The deed upon its face bears every mark & appearance of antiquity equal to its date, purports to be witnessed by two persons both of whom were alive at the date mentioned in the deed, & have been dead for a great number of years, & evidence was given to show that one of the witnesses, who makes his mark was illiterate - Alley one of the parties to the deed was for many years dead or removed & no proof was offered as to his hand writing, & the Signature of Jane Scott was by her mark. No other evidence was given of the [?] this deed this deed had been found amongst Abram Cresons papers after his death evidence was also given to show that the plaintiff had been held in Servitude by Joseph Williams from the time of the Indenture before stated up to his death. The Court in its direction to the Jury instructed them that the Indenture (a Copy of which forms part of the Case) was Prima Facie evidence of freedom & put Joseph Williams & those who claimed under him to the necessity of showing that the pltff was a slave - that as to the damages they were for them to assess - that they ought not to be excessive & extravogant, but reasonable, the costs & trouble in bringing the Suit, & obtaining agents & Council to prosecute it were proper to be considered of by the Jury - and it was also for them to say whether in a Case (if such was the fact) where a person in face of light & knowledge &c nevertheless continued to hold in slavery a being, who from its degraded condition was unable to take measures for its own relief or to enlist the sympathy of others to afford assistance, was not a circumstance of aggravation in the estimation of the damages to eight hundred dollars. On the motion for a new trial when the true state of the Case was ascertained, & the ground for excessive damages was stated, the Court then proposed, that upon this discovery the question of damages shoud be immediately Submitted to the same Jury who had assessed the damages Complained of. The Pltffs counsel consented, but the Defendts. Council declined acceeding to the proposal - the Plfs then remitted the whole of the damages to two hundred & fifty dollars which in the opinion of the Court were reasonable, not being equal as it appears to the Court, to an entire indemnity for the costs & the one years Service under the Defendant after the death of Joseph Williams his testator. The motion for a new trial was overruled & defendt appealed to the Supreme Court.
H.S

Stokes County

The Court in stating the evidence to the Jury said that it was in the power of those who claimed under Joseph Williams to show whether he had ever been out of the possession of Mima the plaintiff from the time of the indenture to his death, that the Pltf offered evidence to show such continued possession at divers times & in different years, & if the Defendt did not show the fact, having it in his power to do, presumption arose that the fact was against him, or he woud have shown it - & that the Defendant had offered no such evidence.

Scott vs Lewis Williams

Melvina Scott   vs Lewis Williams
Jesse Scott   vs Lewis Williams
Sally Scott   vs Lewis Williams

Each of these cases was similar to the case of Jemima Scott vs Lewis Williams. The Plaintiffs are the children of Jemima & gave evidence of it, & also the same evidence of the freedom of their Mother that she gave in her Action. The Defendant gave the same evidence also, with the addition of a bill of Sale from William T Lewis to Joseph Williams in 1792, and a bill of Sale from Abram Creson to William T Lewis in October 1788 before the bringing of the writ of Error in Salisbury Copies of the bills of Sale as also of the record in Salisbury Supr Court form part of these cases. The Jury were instructed that the amount of damages be as a matter peculiar for their consideration, that they might in assessing it take into consideration the difficulty which the Pltffs had to encounter an amount of their Liberation in order to assert their freedom in a Court of Justice. Whether it was necessary to obtain the assistance of friends, & whether they coud be obtained without record given, or promised, and whether the Pltfs had the means of rewarding such assistance. And it was for them to say whether in [?] brought by the Pltf to extricate himself from unjust Slavery which was the cause of his poverty, if such they found the facts to be, they arove in the estimation of his damages, leave him under the necessity of again going into Servitude to remunerate those by whose assistance he had been relieved from an Ilegal State of Slavery - That the damages shoud be reasonable & not extravagant. On similar motion in

Stokes County

the case of Jemima Scot for a new trial it was warranted & appeal to the Supreme Court. The true State of these cases was ascertained to be [?] brought against Lewis Williams for his [?] as Executor after the death of his Testator before the trial commenced.

Stokes County

Chapter Two

Stokes County

Civil Actions

North Carolina State Archives
Stokes County Records
Miscellaneous Slave Records
C.R.090.928.13

Margaret Gittens Vs. George Hauser [1808]
Civil Action
Stokes County, NC

In Equity
Margt. Gittens Vs George Hauzer
Original Bill

Issue one Subpoena, a copy thereof and a copy of this Bill to the Sheriff of Stokes to Serve the Copies on G. Hauzer & to return to Court the Original Sobpoena. Filed in my office Feby 15th 1808
Jas. Parks C.M.E.

Stokes County

To the honorable The Judge in Equity of the Superior Court for the County of Surry --

Humbly Complaining showeth unto your Honor Your Oratrix Margaret Gittens of Surry County Widow That your Oratrix was possessed of divers Slaves as of her own property and being so possessed one Thomas A. Word Contriving and intending to impose upon and deceive and defraud her of her said Slaves produced to her an Instrument in Writing which he falsely fraudulently and deceitfully pretended and affirmed to her was a deed of gift from one Drury Holcomb to him and requested her to witness the same and your Oratrix confiding in his affirmation and then believing the same to be true did sign her name to the same Instrument believing she was only attesting the execution thereof by the said Holcomb as a witness thereto That your Oratrix soon afterwards discovered the fraud by hearing of the said Thomas A. Word's claiming title to her Slaves and then she learnt for the first time that the said Instrument she had subscribed her name to purported to be deed of gift of all or some of her said Slaves from herself to the said Thomas A Word and not a deed from the said Holcomb to him and that the said Holcomb was the witness and herself the party executing the same That George Hauzer of the County of Stokes Esqr. informed her of the Fraud and possessed himself her friend in the warmest and most benevolent terms and spoke of the said Thomas A. Word as a wicked crafty and designing man who had by the means and pretence aforesaid deceived her and intended to cheat and defraud her of her said Slaves and by such and the like conduct the said George Hauzer greatly insinuated himself into your Oratrix's favor and esteem so much that she entertained a very high opinion as well of his honor and integrity as of his friendship for her and believed him a man warm in her interest and welfare from no other motive than pur Benevolence towards her and your Oratrix being a very old and infirm Woman aged Eighty five years and upwards extremely weak as well in her Mind as Body incapable of the management of her Business and Concerns and easily imposed upon and all this being known to the said George Hauzer he the said George Hauzer formed the design of defeating the Fraud intended by Word and of procuring an Appropriation of your Oratrix's Slaves to his own use and Benefit and in order to carry it into execution he spoke largely to her of Words claim aforesaid and his wickedness deceit and ill designs and represented to her that the said Word would certainly sue her for her Slaves upon the said fraudulent deed of Gift and deprive her of all support

Stokes County

and Maintenance in her very advanced time of life and that she would be under great difficulties and must be at great fatigue trouble and expence to prove the Fraud and avoid the same and that the task of such a defence would be far beyond her strength and condition to accomplish and thereupon the said George Hauzer offered his services to effect the same which your Oratrix gratefully accepted and promised to reward him reasonably for the same but this did not satisfy the said George Hauzer who to carry his designs aforesaid into complete effect artfully represented to your Oratrix that she would lose her Slaves if she did not prosecute Word for the forgery and deceit aforesaid and then offered to institute and carry on such a prosecution diligently and faithfully at his own cost and trouble if your Oratrix would give him her Slaves at her death and Your Oratrix then not possessing an understanding adequate to the Business she was then about but totally incapable of transacting the same and being harrassed and uneasy in her Mind and easily imposed upon through its weakness and defects did execute another instrument in writing transferring to the said George Hauzer as he then represented to her and as she then believed all her said Slaves at her death to the end that the said George Hauzer should prosecute the said Word to conviction and avoid the Instrument fraudulently obtained of her as first mentioned and that she might enjoy her said Slaves for her subsistence during her life and Your Oratrix avers that she never received any consideration whatsoever for the said Slaves or any of them or the execution of the Instrument last mentioned That considering how weak harrassed and uneasy your Oratrix was in her mind and how inadequate and incapable of the same was to the Business she last executed at the time of its execution and that she received no consideration whatever she hoped that the said George Hauzer would have delivered up the Instrument last executed to be Cancelled as in Equity and Justice he ought to have done. But now so it is may it please your Honor that the said George Hauzer combining and confederating himself to and with divers other persons at present unknown to your Oratrix whose names when recovered she prays may be inserted and they made parties defendants hereto with apt matter and words to charge them and contriving how to injure and deprive your Oratrix of all benefit whatsoever of the said Slaves hath refused to deliver up the same Instrument to be Cancelled and hath to complete his design aforesaid lately seized upon all the said Slaves and took and carried away the same from and out of the possession your Oratrix and converted and disposed thereof to his own use and thereby left her utterly destitute of all

Stokes County

support and Maintenance whatever pretending that the Instrument she last executed is an absolute deed of Gift of all the said Slaves to the said George Hauzer taking effect from its execution and therefore the property thereof already and immediately vested in him. Your Oratrix charges that if the same Instrument is as above pretended that the same is fraudulent and void in as much as she was deceived by the said George Hauzer believing the same to transfer the property not until her death in possession and not the absolute and immediate property and possession All Which Actings doings and pretence of the said George Hauzer are contrary to equity and good conscience and tend to the manifest wrong and Injury of your Oratrix In tender consideration whereof and for that your Oratrix is utterly remediless by the strict rules of the Common Law and cannot have adequate relief without the aid and assistance of a court of equity where matters of fraud and of this nature are properly cognizable and relievable To the end therefore that the said George Hauzer may upon his corporal oath full true distinct and perfect answer make to all and singular the matters and things herein before set forth as fully and particularly as if the same were here again repeated and interrogated And more especially that he may answer and set forth whether such Instruments as herein before mentioned or any other and what Instruments or Writings or Instrument or Writing and of what dates purport and effect were not made or executed in the manner and under the circumstances herein before in that behalf set forth or how otherwise and whether he did not form such design and make such pretence as herein before set forth or any other and what design or pretence and why and for what reason, And That the said Instrument to the said George Hauzer may be set aside vacated and cancelled and that your Oratrix may be restored to the immediate possession of all the said Slaves and quieted in the possession thereof by this injunction of this honorable Court and that the said George Hauzer may account for and pay your Oratrix for the Hire service and profits thereof in the mean time and that your Oratrix may [Torn] otherwise relieved in the premises as the nature of her case shall require and according to the rules of equity and good conscience. May it please your Honor to grant unto your Oratrix a Writ of Subpoena to be directed to the said George Hauzer thereby commanding him at a certain day and under a certain pain therein to be inserted personally to be and appear before your Honor in this honorable court then and there to answer the premises and to stand to and abide such order and decree therein as to

Stokes County

your Honor shall seem agreeable to equity and good conscience. And your Oratrix shall ever pray &C.

North Carolina } To Thos. Perkins Esqr. and
Surry } Jesse McKiney

Esquires Two of the Justices Assigned to keep the peace in & for the County of Surry Greeting.
Whereas we in Confidence of your prudence & fidelity have appointed you or either of you by an order of the Honorable Court of Equity in the County of Surry Made in A Case Wherein Margaret Gittins is Complt. & George Houser is deft. to Cause to Come before you at such time & place as you think proper Hugh Armstrong Esqr., Robert Poor, & his Wife, Jonathan Unthank to give evidence in the forgoing suit & that you take Such Depositions in Writing & Return the same Sealed Up Under your hands & Seals to our Next Court of Equity to be held for the said County on the first Monday in March Next together With this Writ -- Witness Jas. Parks CM Equity of our sd. Court At office the first Monday in Septr. 1809 & XXXIII year of our Independence.
Jas. Parks CME

State of North Carolina }
Surry County }

Pursuant to a Commission to us Directed from the Clark and Master in Equity for the Superior Court of Surry to take the Deposition of Hugh Armstrong Robert Poore & Jonathan Unthank to be read as Evidence in a Suit now pending in Equity to be holden at Rock in the town of Rockford on the first monday in march Next wherein Margaret Gittings is plantiffe & George Hauser is Defendant, have caused them to appear before us at the house of Thomas Perkins this 2d day of November 1809 and after being duly sworne on the Wholy Evengelist deposeth and sayeth

the Deposition of Hug[?] Armstrong first
Q. 1. by the Deft. was you & Capt Harris left Executor of Richard Gideons Estate - Ans. We was.

Stokes County

Q. 2. did Richard Gettings in his last will & testament bequeath all his Negroes to his wife Margaret Gittings - Ans. he did all the residue of his Estate after his Just debts was paid & legases that he left

Q. 3. by Deft. Had Richard Gittings at that time any blood relations in this Country to your knowledge, & how near they were related - Ans. Richard Gittings told me, Roger Gittings was a Brother of his who lived on stewarts creek in surry County N.C. at that time

Q. 4. by Deft. Was you Sir as an Executor of Richard Gittings Estate not requested by Mrs. Gittings & myself, to be present when the bill of sale of the Negroes was Executed to me - Ans. Squire Hauser & Mrs. Gittings Came down to Kinkenson[?] forg & sent for me & Informe me that Colr. Word had a deed of gift of her Negroes, at which time Mrs. Gittings Engaged with Squire Hauser to Examine the office where it should be recorded to Know the truth of the same, & some few days after Squire Hauser returned to the forge & shewd me a Coppy of a deed of gift for Eleven Negroes, the next day after by the request of Mrs. Gittings I went to her house & meet with Squire Hauser there in presence of both them I read a bill of sale from Mrs. Gittings to Hauser & allso her deed of gift to Word, & requested of her if she had made such a deed of gift to Colr. Word Not to assign the bill of sale to Hauser, as she might envolve them all in law & Injur Word Carecter

Q. 5. by Deft. did not you & Capt Harris as Executors of Richard Gittings deceased, before you ware willing to have the Bill of sale of sd. Negroes Executed to me by Mrs. Gittings demand a bond of me with Conditions that I should be answerable for all Claims against his Estate - Ans. I did

Q. 6. how large was the sum I was bound in & in whose possession is that bond Now - A. I believe it is for one or two thousand Dollars & it is in my possession at this time.

Q. 7. by Deft. would you Now as an Executor be willing to give me up that bond - Ans. I am not

Stokes County

Q. 8. by Deft. did you Consider that I frightend or pursuaded Mrs. Gittings in the best manner to give me a bill of sale of them Negroes - Ans. you did not in my presence

Q. 9. Deft. did she not Insist to have the bill of sale Executed to me for them Negroes - Ans. She did on the principle of Hausers Maintaining of her her lifetime

Q. 10. Deft. was not you one of the subscribing witnesses to said bill of sale & proved it in Open Court - A. I was

Q. 11. Deft. did not Mrs. Gittings in your & Capt. Harris presence deliver them negroes to me as her right & title hand by hand - A. as to my part I saw them Delivered in that manner

Q. 12. Deft. did you & Capt. Harris as Executors object to the delivery of the said Negroes to me - A. I did not as to my part, as I found she was determind to do it, & she did so with a free Voluntary Concent

Q. 13. Deft. are you not Confident that as far as you was acquainted with Mrs. Gittings that at the time of her Executing of said Bill of sale & her Delivery of said Negroes to me she was in her proper Senses - A. she appeared so to me

Q. 14. have you not heard it General said for six or seven years past that the said Negroes was mine - A. No. I allways heard her say she Intend her Negroes for her friends in Ireland & if she Could find them, if not she Expected to give them to some friends she had to the Northward, to a Cousin she had by the name of Jane Martin

Q. 15. Deft. did you not see Mrs. Gitting receive the money specified in the bill of sale, & was I not bound to support her during Life, as a Consideration for said Negroes - A. I did not see the money paid, but the bill of sale specified a support for her during life and Hauser offerd to give her any security for the same, & furnish her with a room & anything Necessery for a person of her [?] she did not require security

Q. 16. Deft. did not James Bryson about that time Mrs. Gittings Executed said Bill of sale to me Come to her house & in what manner did

Stokes County

Bryson behave himself towards me - A. Bryson addressd himself to Capt Harris & my self & after some Conversation some warm words past between Hauser & Bryson

Q. 1. by Plantiffe had you any reason to believe that she would Execute that bill of sale to Hauser had it not been for the attact Colr. Word made on her. - Ans. I believe she would not

Q. 2. by Pltff was the bill of sale that was Executed to Hauser wrote before you got there or after - A. I expect it was wrote before as it was ready when I got there, all Except the blanks & them I filld up by there request

Q. 3. by Plff did she not on that day appeared to be more Confused than at any other time. - A. I think Not

Q. 17. by Deft. when Mrs. Gittings & myself was at the forge & sent for you as an Executor did not I tell her in your presence that if I undertook the Business for her that if I did not recover the Negroes from Word I would pay all Cost & Expence of the suit & still support her hansomly during her life & that it was a risk with me if I recoverd I ought to have something & if I did not recover I was to pay all cost & still support her - A. that Conversation did not pass at the forge in my hearing, but I heard them Expressions from Hauser on the day the bill of sale was Executed

Q. 18. by Deft. did I not on the day Word was on tryal and was acquited, at the house of Thos. Perkins, offer to Mrs. Gittings that if she would pay me for the Expence that I have been at which was trifling, that I would wish to be off from all the Contract - A. you did & she refused of Exepting of it

[Editor's note: The questions skip #19 and resume on #20].

Q. 20. did not Mrs. Gittings at the time of signing sealing & Delivering the Negroes to me Except a Negroe woman Name bett & child moses to be freed at her death on her good behaviour of the laws of North Carolina would admit of it - Ans. She did and further this deponent sayeth Not
Sworne to and subscribed befor us this 2d day of November 1809
Thomas Perkins JP   Hugh Armstrong (Seal)
Jesse McKinney

Stokes County

the Deposition of Jonathan Unthank
Q. 1. by Deft. do you remember of going with me and Peter Hauser to Mrs. Gittings & what was the talk Concerning the Negroes she had give me a bill of sale for - A. I did go with them there and heard Hauser offer to give up to Mrs. Gittings all his Clame against the Negroes, she give him a bill of sale for provided she would give him an indemnified bond against all damages that might arise against him which she refused to do or Except of

Q. 2. by Deft. do you recollect what time this talk was - Ans. I believe it to be the 29th day of August in the year one thousand Eighteen Hundred and Eight

Q. 3. by Deft. did I or did I not request of you to furnesh her with Bacon Corn Shugar Coffee & other Necessarys - Ans. Hauser left money with me and Directd me to furnesh her with such Necessarys as she wanted

Q. 4. Deft. did she receive any articles - Ans. she sometime past she did but has not of late

Q. 5. Did you understand what was the reason - A. I understood that Bryson under took to furnish her was the reason and further this deponant sayeth Not sworne to and Subscribed before us this 2d. day of Novr. 1809
Thomas Perkins JP   Jona. Unthank
Jesse McKinney JP

The deposition of Robert Poor
Q. 1. by Deft. How many years was you with Mrs. Gittings and was you present when she sold & deliverd her Negroes to me - A. I had lived with her two years & was present when she sold & Deliverd her Negroes to you

Q. 2. by Deft. do you believe that Mrs. Gittings was in her perfect sences at that time - Ans. I knew nothing to the Contrary

Q. 3. Deft. did you see me pay her the money specified in the bill of sale, & was she not perfectly satisfyed with the Contract and did she not deliver her Negroes to me hand by hand - Ans. I saw the money paid & she appeard to be satisfyed and saw the Negroes deliverd by her hand by hand

Stokes County

Q. 4. Deft. was you a subscribing witness to the bill of sale - Ans. I was

Q. 5. Deft did you not understand that I was to furnish Mrs. Gittings with a Comfortable Support during her Natural Life, and did I not performe to her satisfaction while she would receive of me - A. I do not recollect during her life, but I recollect of your sendings as long as she would receive

Q. 6. by Deft. when I sent the Negroes with Mr. Perkins into the Hollow were they not Deliverd to you with particular Instructions not to deliver them to any person without an order from me - Ans. the Negroes was deliverd up to me I do not recollect any other particulars

Q. 7. Deft you have seen me often at Mrs. Gittings house did you Ever in my Conduct with Mrs. Gittings discover that I pursuaded or [?] her to sign me a bill of sale for them Negroes - Ans. I have often seen you there but never discoverd any thing of the like and further this deponant sayeth Not sworn to & subscribed before us this 3d day of November in the year of our Lord one thousand Eight Hundred & Nine
Thos Perkins JP   Robert Poor   (Seal)
Jesse McKinny

Commission to take
Depo
Margaret Gittins
Vs.
George Hauser

No Carolina   } To Thomas Perkins & Jesse McKinny
Surry County   } Esqrs

    Two of the Justices Assigned to keep the peace in & for the County of Surry

    Whereas we in Trust & Confidence of your prudence & Fidelity have Appointed you or either of you in Conformity with An Order of Sd.

Stokes County

Court of Equity Lately made in A Case wherein Margaret Gittins is Complt. & George Houser is Deft. to Cause to Come before you At such time & place as you May think proper   David Lain

To give Evidence in Sd. Suit & that you take the same on Oath & in writing & return the same, sealed Up Under your hands & Seals to the Next Court of Equity to be held for this County in the Town of Rockford on the first Monday in Sept. Next - Given under my hand at office the first Monday in March 1810
Jos. Parks CME

                        Commission to take Depo.
                              M Gittins
                                Vs.
                              G Houser

State North Carolina   } Agreeable to a Commission to us
Surry County   } Directed from the Clerk & Master

in Equity for the County of Surry to us directed   Thos Perkins & Jesse McKinney both acting Justices for said County to take the Deposition of David Lain.

to be read as evedence in a Suit Now pending in Our Superior Court of Equity to be holden in the town of Rockford on the first Monday in September Next wherein Margeret Gittings is Plantiff and George Hauser is Defendant, have caused to come before us at the house of Thomas Perkins on the 25th day of August 1810 - and after being duly Sworn on the Holy Evengelist of allmighty God deposeth and Sayeth

Qu. 1 by Agent for Plantiff was you at the house of Margeret Gittings on the day She gave Hauser a bill of Sale for her Negroes. A. I was there Earely in the Morning and George Hauser was there when I went

Qu. 2. by Same. what arguments did Hauser Make use of to her in Order to ocation her to make him a bill of sale for her Negroes. A. the force of his discorse, appeard to be that there was no Other means that She could obtain the Negroes from Word, which she appeard unwilling to do for

Stokes County

fear She would be Cappled out of her Negroes but did agree to give him a bill of sale but do not know on what principles.

Qu. 3. by the Same in what State of mind did She appear to be in Ans. She did not appear to be Capable of doing any business, as She was much flusterated in mind, and further this deponent Sayeth Not.

	his	
Thos. Perkins JP	David X Lain	(Seal)
Jesse McKinny JP	mark	

Margaret Gittin
Vs.
George Houser
Richd. Isbell
Edward Hickman
Caty Poor
Isaac Beldsoe

State of North Carolina } Ss.
Surry County }
To Charles Taliaferro & Thomas Perkins Esquires, Justices assigned to keep the Peace in and for the county of Surry Greeting:

Know Ye, that we in confidence of your prudence and fidelity, have appointed, and bt these presents do give unto you, or either of you, full power and authority, in pursuance of an order from the Judge of our Superior Court in Equity made in a cause wherein, Margaret Gittings is plaintiff & George Hauser defendant, at such time and place as you shall think fit, to take upon oath, on the Holy Evangelist of Almighty God the deposition of Richard Isbill William Hickmon Robert Poore & Caty Poore Edwin Hickmon & Isaac Bledsow touching and concerning what they may know in and about the said controversy; and that you take such deposition in writing, and return the same, closed up under your hand and seal to our said court, to be held for the county of Surry on the first Monday in March next, together with this Writ.

Stokes County

Witness Jas Parks Clerk & Master of the said court, at office the 16 day of Febr. in the XX[Blank] year of American Independence, Anno Domini 1810
Jas. Parks CME

State of North Carolina } Pursuant to a Commission to
Surry County } us directed to

Charles Taliefero and Thomas Perkins, both acting Justices of said County, from the Judge of Said superior Court in Equity to take the deposition of Richard Isbell William Hickmon Edwin Hickmon Isaac Bledsow Robert Poore & wife Catey Poore to be read in Evidence in a suit Now pending in the Superior Court in Equity to be Holden on the first Monday in March Next in the town of Rockford Surry County wherein Margeret Gittings is plantiffe & George Hauser is Defendant Hauser being present & James Bryson who says he is Agent for Margaret have Cause them to Come before us at the House of Thomas Perkins on the 17th day of February 1810 & after being duly sworn on the Holy Evengelist of Allmighty God deposeth and sayeth

       The Deposition of Richard Isbill first

Qus. by Bryson agent for Plantiffe was you acquaint with Margeret Gittings on the first day of May last with regard to her Situation & the reason that Caused her to move from her plantation Ans. I was at Mrs. Gittings about that time which was the day she moved from her plantation She appeard to be in distress for feare Squire Hauser would Come & take her Negroes away as she said she had heard he was Coming for that purpose I then left the place and after Course of an hour oe two returnd she was then fixing to move - She then said her wishes was to stay if she Could and keep her Negroes in peace - Squire Brysons answer to her in that was he thought she might she then said she did not think she could without William Hickmon or myself would under take her Business for her which I refused to do - Squire Bryson Insisted on William Hickmon to Undertake for her, and told him if he would he would make it worth his while, and Allso told him if he Could no make Enough on the plantation to satisfy himself he would satisfy him other ways, Squire Bryson then

Stokes County

told her if she would Content her self to stay he would furnish her with Corn Bacon & any other Necessarys she wanted - she then said without some white man she Could not stay there for they would Come & take her Negroes away

Q. 2. by the same - Was you generally acquaint with Mrs. Gittings from the time Hauser moved the Negroes untill she moved her self Ans. I was often there and made Enquiry in what manner she was liveing, the first time I Enquired she said squire Hauser had sent her some flower & shugar, at a Number of Other times I was there & allways after that told me Squire Bryson supported her and if he had not done it she must perishd

Q. 3. by the same - did she ever express any doubts of beliefe that squire Hauser & Word had Joind to take her Negroes away. Ans. She did and said she believed it to be true & further said she believd Squire Hauser to be as bad a man as Thos. Word

Q. 4. by the same, did you Ever here Mrs. Gittings Express any thing with regard to her wish or Intentions to give Squire Hauser her Negroes Ans. I Never did, but have heard her say that squire Hauser pretended to befrend her but she believd it to be for his own Intrest as he might get her Negroes from her to him self and that he did Not Care if she was dead so he had the Negroes, the above Conversation was past between us at times when she had sent for me to Come to her house - and further this deponant sayeth Not
Thos Perkins JP   Richd. Isbell
Chas Taliaferro JP

The Deposition of Edwin Hickmon

Qus. 1 by James Bryson agent for Mrs. Gittings Did Mrs. Gittings petition you to wright letters for her Ans. She did send for me to wright a Letter to Mr. Mitchel to Come and take her business in hand for she believd that Mr Hauser & Word had Joind to get her Negroes from her; and some time after She Come to see me in Order to wright another letter to or nearely the same purpose as Mitchel had faild to Come, which I did wrighgt for her

Stokes County

Qu. 2. by the same did you Ever understand that Mitchel Comeing upon receiving them letters Ans. I did understand so by Mrs. Gittings & allso understood so on yeasterdy by Mr Mitchel & further this deponant sayeth Not

Chas Taliaferro JP   Edwin Hickmon
Thos Perkins

The Deposition of Caty Poore

Qus. first by James Bryson agent for Plantiffe did you Not live at Mrs. Gittings at the time the first Contract took place between Squire Hauser & Margeret Gittings Concerning the Negroes Now in Dispute. A. I did

Q. 2. by same what reason did Mrs. Gittings assign to you for putting her Negroes in the possession of Hauser - A. She said she was afraid Mr. Word would take them away from her

Q. 3. by same did you believe she put them in the possession of Hauser for feare of Word, or for respect to Hauser, or did you Ever heare her say she Intended to give them to Hauser before that took place Ans. I allowed it was through feare she did it

Q. 4. by the same What reason did you have for telling Mrs. Gittings that Hauser would Come and take the Negroes away the day before she movd Ans. when I was at Court Hauser told me to tell her, I would Come up to see her in a few days & if she was willing he would take the Negroes home with him & if not she might keep them her lifetime that was if Information I gave Mrs. Gittings

Qu. 1. by Deft Mrs Poore how long was you acquaint with Mrs. Gittings Ans. little better than five years

Qu. 2. by Deft did you Ever know her to be delirious or out of her Common reason A. I never did

Qu. 3. by Deft do you recollect of hearing Mrs. Gittings say any thing about making a will A. I do not recollect that I Ever did

Stokes County

Q. 4. by Deft was you present when she sold & deliverd me them Negroes A. I was

Q. 5. by Deft do you know or ever discover that I Ever sceard or pursuaded her to sell or deliver them Negroes to me Ans. No I never did

Q. 6. by Deft when she deliverd them Negroes to me did not she do it with a Voluntary & free Consent Ans. I think she did

Q. 7. by Deft do you know of any thing that I furnishd Mrs. Gittings towards her Support while I had the Negroes in possession Ans. you furnishd her with sugar Coffee & flower

for Plantiffe
Q. by James Bryson agent was not the sugar Coffee & flour sent in the waggon when the Negroes was Carried away A. I believe it was

Q. by the same do you know of any being offerd afterwards A. she told me she had receivd some Coffee & sugar at another time

Q. by the same do you know who found her bread & meat the Insuing year when her [?] provision was out Ans. I do not Know further this deponant sayeth not

Thos. Perkins JP	her
Chas Taliaferro JP	Caty X Poore
	mark

The Deposition of Isaac Bledsow

Qus. first by James Bryson agent for plantiffe was you Not present at Mrs. Gittings when she movd from her plantation A. I was

Q. 2. by the same what reason did she Inform you was the Cause of her moving away from her plantation A. I understood by the Old woman that her Negroes was unruly so that she Could do nothing with them & Mr Bryson had to find her & said she had better move to where it was, than to have to **[Smudged]** after it, & further said she Expected Every Night Squire Hauser would Come & take her Negroes away & said she had kept

Stokes County

them lockt for better than a week for feare he would Come & take them away.

Q. 3. by the same after Mrs. Gittings moved out of the house did you not move in to it Ans. I did

Q. 4. by the same did not Thos. East Hauser's Son in Law & son Come to that house at a dead hour of the Night & open the door Ans. Thos. East had the door open when I waked & said he had made free to open the door & hoped it was no harm & said he wishd from acquaintance to stay all night. I told him that I had gest moved there & was not fixt to Entertain any person - he said he Expected the Old wom[an] was there & came untill he heard to contrary as he Enquired where she was gone. I told him she had moved To Mr Brysons

Q. by Deft what has been Thos East general Character within your knowledge Ans. his general Caracter was an honest peaceable Citizen and further this deponant sayeth not
Chas Taliaferro   Jp   Isaac Bledsoe
Thos. Perkins   Jp

The foregoing depositions sworn to & subscribed before us the day and date before mentiond
Thos Perkins   Jp
Chas Taliaferro   JP

State of No Carolina   } To Thomas Hadly & Charles Christman
Surry County   } Esqrs

Two of the Justices assigned to keep the peace in & for the County of Surry

Whereas we in Confidence of your prudence & fidelity have Appointed you or either of you in Conformity to And order of our Court of Equity made in a Case Wherein Margaret Gittins is Complainant & George Houser is Deft to Cause to Come before you As such Time & place As you think proper   Joshua Roberts & Wife Priscilla Roberts   Thos Longino Robert Poore & Elijah Gillaspie

Stokes County

To give Testimony in Sd. Case & that you take the same Upon Oath & in Writing & return the same Sealed up Under your hands & seals to our Next Court of Equity to be holden for the County of Surry At the Court house in Rockford on the first Monday in Sept. Next together With this Writ

Witness Jas. Parks CME of our Sd. Court At Office the first Monday in March in the year of our Lord 1810 & XXXIV year of our Independance
Jas. Parks CME

State of North Carolina }
Surry County }

In Complyance to Commission to us Directed from the Clerk & Master in Equity for the County of Surry to take the Deposition of Joshua Roberts Priscilla Roberts Thos Longino Robert Poore Elijah Gillaspie we have met accordingly at the house of Jesse Lesters on the 6th day of Sept. 1810 which depositions is to be read in Evidence in a suit Now pending in the Superior Court of Equity to be Holden at the town of Rockford on the first Monday in September Next wherein Margeret Gittings is Complaninent & George Hauser is Defendant & after beig duly Sworne on the Holy Evengelist of allmighty God deposeth and sayeth

The Deposition of Joshua Roberts first
Qut. 1. by James Bryson Agent for Complainant What conversation did you hear pass between the present complainant, & defdt., at your House on or about the first of July 1810
Ansr. George Hauser came to my House & took Miss Gittins out to the Chimney end of the House & had private Conversation with her an Hour or longer, after which Hauser came in & asked for pen & ink, as he wanted to write notices, he then went on to write something, Hauser & Miss Gittins went into priate again & afterward Peter Hauser came & requested me to go & see what they had done, I did so, & Hauser handed me a paper with Miss Gittens Name assigned at the bottom, I looked over it, the contents were this (as Hauser read it to me) it was a direction to the Clerk & master in Equity to dismiss the suit Miss Gittens had against him & if any Costs arise from Said Suit he Hauser was to discharge the Whole,

Stokes County

& also to Discharge Js Bryson from the Agency of Miss Gittens I wished it kept a Secret
In the Evening Miss Gittins appeard to be very uneasy for what was past, Hauser came to me next morning & told me he discoverd an uneasiness in Miss Gittins, & that if she was uneasy he would destroy the Instrument of Writing he had Rec'd from her - but rather concluded to let the Instrument of Writing Stand as it was -- On Hauser starting, She wished to have the paper Deposited in my hands, which Hauser refused, She then wanted the paper Destroyed & Hauser Said he would destroy it took a paper out of his pocket & tore it to pieces, which he said was the paper Miss Gittins had assigned -- & Further this Deponant saith not

The Deposition of Pryscilla Roberts

Quest. 1st Was, or Was Not, Miss Gittins at the time of Hausers before mentioned private contracting with her, on the first of July, in a state of Intoxication by Spiritous Liquors so as to render herv incapable of much or any business.
Ansr. I believe she was under the influence of Spirits, when the business was done

Quest. 2. Whose Spirits did she become intoxicated with
Ansr. With Hausers Spirits

Quest. 3. Is She Accustomed to Intoxication by Spirits or was it from Hausers influence She became intoxicated
Ansr. I believe it was by Hausers Influence at that time she became intoxicated & further this deponant saith Not
Sworn & Subscribed before us } Joshua Roberts
CS Crissman JP } priscilla Roberts
Thos Hadby   JP

The Deposition of Elijah Gillaspie

Quest. 1st What was Hausers expressions to you concerning the Negroes he got of Miss Gittens
Ansr. I was at Hausers House, and he stated to me all he had done was out of friendship to Miss Gittens, that he did not intend keeping the Negroes longer than Miss Gittens got an Heir, that he kept an account of what Money he expended in her behalf & that he only intended to be

Stokes County

repaid his Money again, & he also be paid for his trouble & further this Deponent Saith not
Sworn to & Subscribed before us

CS Crissman   JP   }
Thos. Hadby   JP   } Elijah Gillaspie

We do hereby certify that the before mentioned Depositions were taken by consent of parties James Bryson Agent for Complainant, & Henry Houser, Agent for Defdt, were present
Test.
CS Crissman JP
Thos. Hadby JP

Agreeably to a Commission to us Directed from the Superior Court of Equity for the County of Surry. We have this day Caused personally to appear before us in the Town of Rockford at the house of Matthew M Hughs Isaiah Coe to declare on Oath what he may know in a Certain Matter of Controversy to be read in Evidence in said matter now pending in said Court between Margaret Gittins plaintiff and George Hauser Dft. and after being duly Sworn Deposes and says as follows.

Question by Jas. Bryson (agent) Please relate the Conversation that passed between you and George Houser respecting the Negroes of Widow Gittins on which said Houser held a claim
Ans. Mr. Houser informed me that Thos A Word had a claim on said Negroes and it was in the power of Word to have carried them off and have left Mrs. Gittins to Suffer because she appeared friendly; She applied to him (G Houser) to befriend her, He informed me he was not anxious to do it, he then said that he had Advised her to make choice of Some Characters in the hollow, which refused to act for her and pressed the business on him (Geo Houser) which she did, and made him a Deed of Gift for said slaves But said Houser said that he had told her that at any time that she would pay him his money expended and his trouble in befriending her concerning said slaves that he would willingly give them up to her again and would leave it to any good men that were Judges to decide between them, for his time costs Sworn to and Subscribed before us this 14th Feby 1811

Stokes County

Test   Says Isaiah Coe
Jonth Haines JP
Ro. C Donl[?]

From the Court of Equity
of the County of Stokes
to
the Clk & Master in Equity
for the County of Surry
Certeriori
made known, transcript transmitted accordingly
to Oct 1812

this Writ must be transmitted with the record
E.S. CME
Sealed Ap 20 1812

Margaret Gideon }
   Vs
Geo Hauser   } Stokes Court of Equity Apl Term 1812

To [Blank] Parks Esquire Clk and Master in Equity for Surry County
It being shewn to our Stokes Court of Equity that the above case was transmitted to us from Surry - and it being further shewn that the record was not completely transferred it is ordered by the Court that a Certiorori issue to the Clk and Master of Surry County, commanding him to send to our next Court to be held the 3d Monday after the 4th Monday of Sept next 1812 a complete record of the case as it stands upon your Dockets that is to say a complete record of all the rules interlocutory Orders & Decrees in said suit had & taken when said suit was depending in the Superior Court of Equity for the County of Surry stating when the Bill & Answer was filed &c &c, whether the case stands for hearing &c &c & all other things related to this case which remain in your custody - You are therefore commanded to transmit the above said Exemplifications & records under your hand & seal, at or before the time mentioned, that further thereof we may cause to be done that which of rights ought to be

Stokes County

done   Witness Emanuel Shober Clk & Master in Equity for Stokes County the 3d Monday after the 4th Monday of March 1812
Emanuel Shober   CME

The deposition of Heriam Gurhart of lawfull age who being first sworn on the Holy Evangelists of Almighty God deposeth & saith that about the last of April or the first of May a Certain Thomas McKinsey & others came to the House of this deponants fathers & stated that Squire Houser was coming for Mrs. Gittins - when Leonard Gearhart, this deponants father, said to the said McKinsey what is that to your business - the said McKinsey replied I made it my business to go & let Squire Houser know where the old woman was - upon which this deponants Mother said that they should not have the old lady, where the said Mckinsey replied, that he would be damned to Hell if they did have her - Soon after which came Squire Houser & a young woman with him & began to converse with Mrs. Gittings about taking her away - this deponant further states that he never heard Mrs. Gittings consent to go with Squire Houser - he also states that in the course of the conversation there arose a dispute concerning the present plaintiff Mitchell - & it was carried to such length that the said McKinsey asked my Brother if he wished to stand in the Shoes of the said Mitchell - that if he did - & would step into the yard - he the said McKinsey would satisfy him - & then Squire Houser told the negroe man who was with him to take up the old Woman & put her into his carriage which was done & they drove away - this deponant further states - that from what he himself hath seen & afterwards heard, & which he believes to be an undoubted truth, that Squire Houser & those others who were with him conspired together to defraud the present plantiff Mitchell of his just rights - this deponant further states that during the time Mrs. Gittings was at his fathers no instrument of writing was ever sent by the old lady to Squire Houser requesting her removal, & that if any such came into the possession of Squire Houser - this deponant believes it was contrived by some designing person - & further this deponant saith not
Hiram Gearhart

Virginia
    Franklin County to wit   the above deposition taken - Subscribed & sworn to at the House of Henry Callaways between the hours of 12 Oclock in the forenoon & 4 Oclock in the afternoon on Saturday the 27th

Stokes County

day of March 1813 before us Justices of the peace for the County aforesd. - Given under our hands & seals the day & year as above stated
                         [?] [?] JP   (Seal)
                         Thos Thompson JP (Seal)

The deposition of Leonard Gearhart of lawful age, who being first sworn on the Holy Evangelist of Almight God deposeth & saith - that about the first day of Decembr. in the year of our Lord one thousand Eight hundred & eleven the Plaintiff Robt. Mitchell on his return from Panselvania to Carolina called at my house, accompanied with a very elderly & infirm old woman, by the name of Margaret Gittings - who, by her own consent - the said Mitchell left my house, under my care & protection - that the said Margaret Gittings - appeared to be well pleased & satisfied as could be expected of a Woman of her age til about the 15th of Febuary following - when the old Lady was taken sick - & became so much indisposed that this deponant did not expect her to live - during which time the old Lady became much dissatisfied but that dissatisfaction appeared to proceed from the absence of the said Mitchell - whom she stated to be her only relation & friend - that at the request of Mrs. Gittings - this deponant went to Carolina after the said Mitchell - & informed him of the indisposition of the old Lady - as also her request that he should come and see her - that in a short time after, the said Mitchell came to my house, when Mrs. Gittings appeared to be well satisfied - & that at the time the said Mitchell left my house the old Lady was not in a situation to be moved by any person - this deponant further states that about the last of April or the first of May following a Certain Thomas McKinsey & others came to the house of this deponant & informed him that Squire Houser had come after Mrs. Gittings - soon after which Houser himself came & stated that he had come for Mrs. Gittings & after some very rough language, the words I do not certainly recollect the said Houser told a negro man, whom he brought with him - to take up Mrs. Gittings - & place her in the carriage which was done - & the carriage was driven of with the old Lady - this deponant further states - that from what he himself hath seen, & what he hath been informed which he believes to be an undoughted truth - that George Houser and those others who was with

Stokes County

him, had combined together to defraud the plaintiff Robert Mitchell of his just rights, & further this deponant sayeth not.

Leonard Gearhart

Virginia
Franklin County to wit - Subscribed & Sworn to at the House of Henry Callaways between the Hours of 12 oClock in the forenoon & 4 Oclock in the afternoon on Saturday the 27th day of March 1813 - before us Justices of the Peace for the County aforsd. Given under our hands & seals the day & year as above written

       [?] [?] JP   (Seal)
       Thos Thompson JP (Seal)

Mitchel & Gideon
Vs
Hauser

G Hauser to Jesse Kirby

Thomas Yarrel
Michael Hauser
Isaac Bones
Eliz Roya
& others
12 Aug

No Carolina, Stokes County Court of Equity

Peter Hauser maketh Oath, that he deliverd a true Copy of the within Note to Jesse Kirby on the 2d day of July 1813.
Sworn to and subscribed
before me this **[Faded]** day of Aug 1813 Emanuel Shober CME

Mr Jesse Kirby
  Sir
    Youl please to take Notice that on the thirteenth & fourteenth day, of August next at the Tavern in Bethany No Carolina Stokes County I shall proceed to take the deposition of Thomas Yarrell,

Stokes County

Isaac Boones, Michael Hauser, Elisabeth Royer, & others, to be read in Evidence in the suit of Equity, now pending in Stokes County No Carolina wherein Margaret Gittins is Pltff & myself defendant, when & where you may attend to cross examine if you see cause
yours &c &c George Hauser
July 18th 1813

Geo Hauser
to
Jes Kirby

Thomas Perkins
Saml Laurens
Jonath. Unthank
Wellcom Garret & others

Gideon & Mitchell
&
Hauser

Mr Jesse Kirby
    Sir Youl please to take Notice, that at the house of Jonathan Unthank, in Surry County No Carolina on the 19th & 20th & 21st days of August next I shall proceed to take the Depositions of Thoms. Perkins Esqr., Samuel Laurenz, Jonathan Unthank, Wellcombe Garret & others, to be read as Evidence in the Suit of Equity, pending in Stokes County No Carolina, wherein Margaret Gittins is Pltff & myself Defendant, when & where you may attend to cross examine if you see cause yours &c &c
Geo. Hauser
July 19th 1813

No Carolina Stokes County, Court of Equity - Peter Hauser maketh Oath, that he deliverd a true Copy of the within Notice to Jesse Kirby, on the 20th of July 1813
Sworn & Subscribed before me
this 3d August 1813   P. Hauser
Emanuel Shober CME

Stokes County

Served a true Coppy of this Notice on Jesse Kirby on the 20 day Day of July 1813
P. Hauser

Hauser Notice
Jesse McKinny
Saml. Laurence
Richd Pucket & others
7, 8, 9 Oct 1813

Mr Jesse Kerby
    Sir,
        Please to take notice that on the Seventh, eighth, & ninth of October next I shall proceed to take the depositions of Jesse McKinny Esqr Thomas Perkins Esqr Samuel Laurence, Richard Puckett, Welcome Garrett and others, at the House of Jonathan & William Unthank in Surry County, State of North Carolina to be read in evidence in a Suit now depending in the Court of Equity Stokes County Wherein Margaret Gittins is Plaintiff & myself Defendant, where you may attend & cross examine if you see cause

                  Your Most Obt Servt.
Sept. 8th 1813   George Hauser

Oct 18 1813 Charles Banner maketh Oath that he deliverd a true Copy of the within Notice unto Jesse Kirby on the 8th day of September 1813
Sworn to before me   C. Banner
Emanuel Shober CME

A Copy of this Notice was delivered to Jesse Kerby at Rockford 8th Sept. 1813 by me
                  C Banner

Depos

Thomas Perkins

Stokes County

Richard Pucket
Oct 7th 1813

State of North Carolina }
Surry County }

In Pursuance to a Commission to us directed Jacob McCraw[?] & George Kincanon both acting Justices for said County, from the Clerk and Master in Equity for the County of Stokes &C to take the deposition of Thos. Perkins & Richd Puckett to be read in evidence in a Suit now pending in the Superior of Equity, in the County of Stokes N.C. wherein Margaret Giddings is plantiff & George Hauser is Deft have Caus him to Come before us at the house of Jonathan Unthanks in said County on the ninth October 1813, & after being duly Sworn on the Holy Evangelist of Almighty God deposeth & sayeth

Quest 1st By Deft How long have you been acquainted with Margaret Giddans Ansr. I have had some acquaintance with her for Seven or Eight Years.

Quest. 2nd by same did you or did you not consider her possessed of common understanding Ansr. I never discovered any thing to the contrary

Quest 3 by same Have you not Seen Mrs Gitians several times while she was at my House Ansr. I have seen her there two or three times.

Qt. 4th by same did she not always seem anxious to talk with you when you saw her Ansr. She did the first time I saw her there particularly

Qt. 5th How did you consider her Mind then Ansr. I did not discover any thing seem to indicate a want of common understanding

Qt. 6th by same What was the conversation you had with her at my House Ansr. I do not recollect the particulars she said Mr Mitchell had taken her with him to his Mothers in the State of Pennsylvania and wanted to give him the slip & Leave him there & complaind that she was unkindly treated, & wishd to return that he started back with her but

Stokes County

Swore she should not see N Carolina again, I also saw him at her own house some short after Esqr Hauser had recd the negroes, she then stated he (Esqr Hauser) had treated her very kindly & shewd me some articles he had sent her towards her support

Quest. 7th by Mr Kirby did not Mrs Gittans state to you that the family with whom Mr Mitchell left her in Virginia did treat her as well as their circumstances seemd to admit Ansr. She did not seem to Exclaim against the people but said they were too poor to furnish her with suitable accommodations in consequence of which she sufferd a good deal.

Qt. 8th by same would you or would you not, if you had have been an Heir to Mrs Gitians Estate viewing her conduct in conveying the same property, to so many different persons for such small considerations have acted as a guardian or have had one appointed to take care of that Estate Ans. I do not Know what I should have done in a case of that kind as I never have studied anything about getting property in that way.

Quest. 9th by same What is thought to be the age of Mrs. Gittians Ans. I have heard some allow she was Eighty or ninety years of age
Sworn to & subscribed before us   Thos. Perkins   (Seal)
the day & date above
Jacob McCraig   (Seal)
Geo Kincannon JP   (Seal)

Richd. Puckett after being duly sworn on the Holy Evengelist of Almighty God deposeth saith as follows (to wit)
Quest. 1 by Deft. How long have you been acquainted with Mrs. Gitians, & have you not always considered her as a woman of sound mind & understanding & have you not seen her at my house & had a good deal of talk with her there Ans. I suppose I have been acquainted with her about twenty years & always considered her possessd of as good understanding as other old women I have also seen her at your House & conversed with her there, & that she seemd to retain her understanding as well as could be expected from her age

Qus. 2d by Kirby From viewing Mrs. Gitians conduct in conveying her property to different persons for the inconsiderable sums for which she

Stokes County

has do you believe her to be in a capacity fitting to trade or transact business of so great importance as the value of her negroes. Ans. I believe there are but few women capable of transacting such business
This deponent further saith not   Richd. Puckett (Seal)
Sworn to & subscribed in presence of us
Geo Kincannon JP   (Seal)
Jacob McCraig[?]   (Seal)

Stokes County   } Ss.

     I Charles Banner Sheriff of said County do hereby Certify that I Summoned qualified & attended the Jury whose names are Signed & Sealed within at the time & place therein mentiond
Given under My hand & Seal
                 C Banner Shff   (Seal)

State of North Carolina   }
Stokes County   }

     In obedience to an order Issued from the Honerable Court of Equity for the County aforesaid I have this 26th day of November AD 1814 Convened in person the following Jurymen unconnected by affinity or Consanguinity with Margaret Gideons at the place of residence of said Margaret in Bethania with Jonathan Dalton, Elijah Hooper, Samuel Shoope, Gottlirb Rank, Abram Transou, Francis Stanter, Adam Buttner, Michl Hauser, William Kraubs, Jacob Lash, & Isaac Bonn & Samuel Vest good & lawful men by me summoned to enquire into the Mind of said Margaret Gittions. We being Sworn on the holy Evengelist of Almighty God to enquire into the Mind of said Margarett Report our Virdict as follows, that she is at this time of good sound mind & Memory & understanding from the Examination we have Strictly made of her Given under our hands & Seals the date above written

Jonathan Dalton	(Seal)	Francis Stanter	(Seal)
Elijah Hooper	(Seal)	Michael Hauser	(Seal)
Samuel Shoope	(Seal)	William Grabs	(Seal)
Gottleb Ranke	(Seal)	Jacob Lash	(Seal)
Abraham Transou	(Seal)	Isaac Bonn	(Seal)

Stokes County

Adam Buttner   (Seal)   Samuel Vest   (Seal)

Affidavit of
Esqr Doub & Esqr Kinnamen

State of North Carolina }
Stokes County   }

    John Doub and Samuel Kinnamen make oath that they with Thomas Lugina[?] as Commissioners took sundry depositions in the suit in Equity, Margaret Gideon against George Hauser, on the 14th day of August 1813, and that they intended to annex a Certificate to the Commissiones, certifying the time and place when and where the said depositions were taken; and the said John Doub saith that he accordingly wrote such certificates, and it was annexed to the said Commissions, but appears not to have been signed by the Commissioners - These Deponents further say that they know of no reason why the said Certificate was not signed, and believes the omission arose from mere inattention, and no other cause

Sworn to and subscribed before   Saml Kinnaman
me this 20 April 1814   John Doub
Emanuel Shober CME

To the Sheriff of Stokes County
Writ. to enquire into the mind
of Mrs. Gideons
Executed & report filed
C. Banner Shff

My fees for this Service is
£1..4..0

State of North Carolina }
Stokes County   } in Equity

To the Sheriff of said County Greetings

Stokes County

You are herewith commanded to sumon a jury of twelve good and Lawfull unconnected with the party by consanguinity or affinity to examine into and with them proceed to the residence of Margaret Gideons then & there to examine and a report to make upon the state of mind of the said Margaret Gideons, and the report then taken legally and properly attested by the jury to be sumoned by you, to return to our next Court of Equity to be holden for the County of Stokes at the Court House in Germanton on the third Monday after the fourth Monday in March next together with this Writ, and this you shall in no wise omit at your peril

    Witness Emanuel Shober Clerk and Master of our said Court at Office the third Monday after the fourth Monday in September AD 1814 and 39th of our Independence
Emanuel Shober CME

Whether sound or not

Office of Court of Equity
Geo Hauser
Fi Fa
to Apl 1819
Satisfied the 12th day of [?]emr 1818
Wm Bays[?] Shff

State of North Carolina

    To the Sheriff of Stokes County, Greeting.

You are hereby commanded that the goods & chattels, lands & tenements of George Hauser if to be found in your County, you cause to be made the sum of twenty five pounds seventeen shillings & ten pence which was adjudged against him for costs, and charges in a suit lately determined in our Court of Equity, held for the County of Stokes, wherein Margaret Gittens was Complainant and George Hauser defendant: whereof the said George Hauser was convicted and liable, as appear to us of record: And have you the said monies before the Judge of our next Court of Equity to be held for Stokes County, at Germanton, on the third Monday after the

Stokes County

fourth Monday in March next, then and there to render unto the Clerk's Office the monies aforesaid, together with this writ.

Witness, Eml. Shober, Clerk & Master of our said Court, at Office, the third Monday after the fourth Monday of September Anno Domini 1818
Emanuel Shober CME

****

Isaac Evans Vs. John Odeneal [1822]
Civil Action
Stokes County, NC

Notice for Jno Odeneal
A Copy delivered the 12th of Decr.
1822
C.L. Banner Shf
by Jno Banner Ds
Mr. John Odeneal

Take notice that on the Monday and Tuesday the third and fourth of February next at the dwelling house of Patrick Gibson in the district of Abbeville and State of South Carolina I shall take the depositions of Samuel Oriply, Higason Matheson, William Truitt and others and on the fourteenth and fifteenth of the same month at the dwelling house of Stern Simmons in the County of Lincoln and State of Georgia I shall take the depositions of John Simmons, Stern Simmons senr and Stern Simmons Jur. and others - all of which will be offerred in evidence in the Suit now pending between us in Stokes County court in which I am plaintiff and you are defendant
Isaac Evans
by attorney

Isaac Evans
Vs.
John Odeneal

Stokes County

To Matthew R. Moore Esqr
Clerk of Stokes County Court
State of North Carolina

State of North Carolina.
To John McDowell & James E. Todd Esquires, Justices assigned to keep the Peace for Lincoln County, and State of Georgia

Know ye, that we reposing special confidence in your fidelity and prudent circumspection, do authorise and empower you, or any of you, that at such time and place as you shall appoint, you call and cause to come before you Sterne Simmons Sen. John Simmons and Sterne Simmons jr. and them diligently examine on the Holy Evangelists of Almighty God, what they may know in and about a certain matter of controversy, now at issue in our County Court of Pleas and Quarter Sessions for the County of Stokes wherein Isaac Evans is Plaintiff, and John Odeneal is Defendant, as well on the part of the Plaintiff as the Defendant, and such examination and deposition by you taken, you are to send certified and enclosed, under your hands and seals, to the next Court to be held for said county, at the Court House in Germanton on the second Monday in March next: and this you shall in no wise omit.

Witness, Matthew R. Moore Clerk of our said Court, the 2d. Monday of December in the 47th year of our Independence, Anno Dom. 1822

Matthew R. Moore CC

Georgia }
Lincoln County }

In obedience to the annexed Commission, to us directed we have met at the house of Sterne Simmons Sen. of the County and State aforesaid and proceeded to take the depositions of the following persons viz Sterne Simmons Sen, John Simmons, & Sterne Simmons jr, at the house of the said Sterne Simmons Sen, on the 15th day of February 1823 to be read as evidence in a Suit depending in the County Court of Stokes, North Carolina, who being duly sworn deposeth & saith as follows:

deposition of Sterne Simmons Senr

Stokes County

On the 24th of March in the year 1822 as well as I can remember, John Odeneal brot to my house a negro fellow named George, which my son John Simmons had partially bought from him - Odeneal himself continued at my house, as well as my memory serves me, the most of the time, untill the morning of the 29th of the same month: the negro fellow George continued at my house all that time: whilst there, the negro fellow complained of being sick - I twice put him to work, once in picking up rocks, & once in sprouting up small bushes: but he was unable to do either, as he said he was, & appeared to me quite unwell - Odeneal, I beleave [?] him unwell, as he gave him while at my house a dose of Castor oil.

deposition of John Simmons

About the 16th day of March 1822, I made a partial Contract with John Odeneal in Vienna, State of South Carolina, for a negro man by the name of George about twenty two years old as stated by said Odeneal, and took the negro home with me, and was to have time to go to Augusta to procure money to pay for him & others, which I purchased at the same time. About the 24th of the same month, the negro complained of being sick, at which time Odeneal was at my house, and at his request I bled the negro, called George appeared better. That day I started to Augusta & Odeneal took the negro fellow George & went to my fathers on the same day, where he could be better attended to in my absence. On the 27th of the same month I returned home by the way of my father's - there found Odeneal & also the negro sick with fever. I therefore determined not to take the negro George, & so stated to Odeneal: the next day, saw the negro again at my fathers upon appearance he was sick

Deposition of Sterne Simmons jr

I saw a negro fellow by the name of George which John Odeneal had some days in March 1822, at my father's Sterne Simmon's senr & the same that my brother John Simmons had partially bought from said Odeneal, and I afterwards [Faded] negro in the possession of Isaac Evans, who had called on me to go to South Carolina where he lived, to see the negro & to see whether it was the same which Odeneal had at my fathers, & which my brother John had partially purchased as before stated, when I saw the negro at Evan's he was sick in bed, between the 9th & 12th of

Stokes County

April of the same year 1822 & I knew that he was the same negro, George, that Odeneal had at my father's.

Taken, subscribed & sworn
to before us this 15th day
of February 1823
John McDowell JP
James E. Todd JP

his
Sterne X Simmons
mark
John Simmons
Sterne Simmons Junr

Isaac Evans Vs John Odeneal
To Matthew R Moore Esqr.
Clerk of Stokes County Court
State of North Carolina
Saml. Perrin TQ
Patrick Gibson JP

State of North Carolina
  To Saml Perrin & Patrick Gibson Esquires, Justices assigned to keep the Peace for Abbeville District County, and State of South Carolina
  Know ye, that we reposing special confidence in your fidelity and prudent circumspection, do authorise and empower you, or any of you, that at such time and place as you shall appoint, you call and cause to come before you Higgason Matheson William Trewett Wm Raney & Dr Saml. Presley and them diligently examine on the Holy Evangelists of Almighty God, what they may know in and about a certain matter of controversy, now at issue in our County Court of Pleas and Quarter Sessions for the County of Stokes wherein Isaac Evans is Plaintiff, and John Odeneal is Defendant, as well on the part of the Plaintiff as the Defendant, and such examination and deposition by you taken, you are to send certified and enclosed, under your hands and seals, to the next court to held for said county, at the Court in Germanton on the second Monday in March next: and this you shall in no wise omit.
  Witness, Matthew R. Moore, Clerk of our said Court, the 2d Monday of December in the 47th year of our Independence, Anno Dom. !822
       Matthew R. Moore CCC

Stokes County

South Carolina   }
Abbeville District }

In obedience to the annext Commission to us directed we have met at the house of Patrick Gibson Esqr in the state and district aforesaid and proceded to take the depositions of the following persons (viz) Higgason Matheson Wm Truett Wm Raney & Dr Saml Presly on Tuesday the 4th February 1823 to be read as evidence in a Suit depending in the County Court of Stokes North Carolina who being all duly sworn deposeth and saith as follows--

the deposition of Higgason Matheson

Who states that John Simmons of Georgia Lincoln County Bought of John Odeneal about the sixteenth or seventeenth of March 1822 a negro man named George that on the 28 or 29 of said month he saw the said Negro at Mathesons ferry on little river and asked said negro if he did not belong to John Simmons John Odeneal made answer and said that he was the same negro and the reason Why John Simmons did not keep him was because he the said negro was taken sick and about the 11th or 12th of April 1822 he saw the said negro in the possession of Isaac Evans verry sick understood that in a few days after he died

Sworn to and subscribed this   Higgason Matheson
4th day of February 1823 befour us
Saml Perrin   Jp   (Seal)
Patrick Gibson   JP   (Seal)

the deposition of Williams Trewett

Who states that he saw negro George on the 29th March 1822 in the possession of John Odeneal who said that he was a citizen of North Carolina we had some conversation about the price of said negro He said to Odeneal that he thought his negro was sick Odeneal made some answer which he does not recollect On the evening of the same day the said Odeneal and Isaac Evans came to his House where the said Evans paid said Odeneal five Hundred and twenty five Dollars for said negro George and the said Odeneal Acknowledged the Anext Bill of Sale in his presence and that he subscribed his name as witness to the same he also in the course of ten or fifteen days frequently saw the said negro George at said Evanses verry Sick that he believes that he was carefully attended to by the said Evans and family while in his illness he also saith that he

Stokes County

would not have given the same attendance that the said Evans and family did give to said negro for less than one hundred dollars also saith that he was present at the Interment of said negro about three weeks after the said Evans purchased him
Sworn to and Subscribed this
4th day of February 1823 before us   Wms. Truitt
Saml. Perrin   JP   (Seal)
Patrick Gibson   JP   (Seal)

Jn Odeneal
to
Isaac Evans
Bill of Sale
Negro George

Abbeville District   South Carolina

       Received Isaac Evans the sum of five Hundred & twenty five Dollars in full Consideration for a Certain Negro man slave by the Name of George the Rights and Title to said slave to said Evans I will Warrant and forever Defend agt. all and Every person or Persons Whatsoever and agt. the Claim of myself my heirs Executors & assigns Witness my hand & seal this 29th March 1822
Test Wms Truitt
                 Jno. Odeneal   (Seal)

South Carolina   }
Abbeville District   }

Before me the subscribing Justice Personally came Williams Truitt who being duly sworn Saith that John Odeneal did in presence of him the deponent Acknowledge the hand and seal above mentioned as his for the use and purpose contained in the above bill of Sale
to this 8th day of Novr. 1822   Wms Truitt
in presence of Patrick Gibson JP

the deposition of Wm Reney who states

Stokes County

That he lived with Isaac Evans in the year 1822 and on or about the 29 of March in the same year that said Evans bought a negro man named George from one Odeneal that on the evening of the same day the said negro complained of being Sick and that on the day following he was put to cuting of fire wood that he complained of being Sick and quit work and continewed Sick untill he died which was about three [days] after Mr Evans purcheced him that he was well attended to in his Illness untill his death

Sworn to and Subscribed before us
the 4th February 1823   William Rainey
Saml. Perrin   JP   (Seal)
Patrick Gibson   JP   (Seal)

    The deposition of Dr Saml Presly who Saith
  That he was called on by Isaac Evans on the 4th of April 1822 to visit a negro man named George which he understood that the said Evans had some time previously purchsed from John Odeneal that he found him very Sick with the billious inflamatory F[Smudged] and he believes from the Simptoms that the disease that he had died with had been for Eight or nine days Standing when he first saw him and that the Symptoms were [Torn] and billious diarrhea and considers that his glan[Smudged] [Smudged]ston was affected with a Cronie disease called Scoffuers [Torn] & that it had produced an enlargement of his glands generally and that he did attend on him attentively and that he died on the Eighteenth of the same month and that his bill for attendence on Said negro George amounted to fourteen dollars and 50 cents that the family of Isaac Evans attended on him Cearfully

Sworn to and Subscribed
before us the 4 February 1823   Samuel Pressly
Saml. Perrin   JP   (Seal)
Patrick Gibson   JP   (Seal)

Isaac Evans
Vs
Jno Odeneal
A copy delivered June 10th 1823

Stokes County

CL Banner Shf

Mr John Odineal
    Take notice that on the 18th and 19th of July next at the house of Patrick Gibson in Abbeville districts South Carolina I shall take the depositions of William Rainey James Leard and others to be read in evidence in my behalf in the Suit now pending in Stokes County Court wherein I am plaintiff and you are defendant
Yours
Isaac Evans
by
James Charter Jr his Atto

Isaac Evans Vs John Odeneal
To Matthew R Moor Esqr
Clerk of Stokes County
Court State of North Carolina

Evans Vs Odeneal
Depo.

State of North Carolina }
Stokes County   }

    To Saml. Perrin and Patrick Gibson Esqrs Justices appointed to keep the peace for Abbeville District & State of South Carolina
    Know ye that we reposing special trust & confidence in your fidelity & prudent circumspection do authorise & empower you or any of you that at such time & place as you shall appoint you call & cause to come before you William Raney and James Lard and there diligently examine on oath what they may know in and about a certain matter of controversy now at issue in our court of pleas & quarter sessions for the County aforesaid wherein Isaac Evans is plaintiff and John Odeneal defendant: as well on the part of the plaintiff as defendant and such deposition by you so taken you shall send certified & enclosed under your hands & seals to our next Court to be held for our said county at the Court house in Germanton on the 2nd Monday of September next and this you shall in no wise omit

Stokes County

Witness Matthew R Moore clerk of our said court at office the 2nd Monday June 1823 & 47th year of Independence
Matt R Moore CCC

South Carolina }
Abbeville District }

In obedience to the annexed Commission to us directed We have met at the house of Patrick Gibson Esqr in the State and District aforesaid and proceeded to take the Depositions of the following persons (to wit) William Rainy and James Leard at the house of the said Patrick Gibson on the 19th day of July 1823 to be read as Evidence in a suit depending in the County Court of Stokes North Carolina who both being duly sworn deposeth and saith as follows

Deposition of Wm Rainy
 Who states on oath that he saw John Odeneal at the house of Isaac Evans on the 29th day of March 1822 with a negro man named George proposing to sell said negro to Isaac Evans recommending of said negro as being a sound negro and a negro much to be depended upon and upon said recommendation the said Evans purchaced him on the said day Also after the purchace on the same evening he heard Odeneal frequently repeat that said George was a sound negro and that Mr. Evans had goten good **[Smudged]**

Deposition of James Leard
 Who states that he saw John Odeneal on the 29th day of March 1822 at the house of Isaac Evans that Odeneal offered to sell a negro man named George whome he recommended as being a healthy and sound negro on that recommendation Isaac Evans purchaced the said negro that on the evening of the same day after the purchace was made he heard him say that Isaac Evans had **[Smudged]** him five hundred and Twenty five dollars also that the negro was a sound negro and that Evans had gotten a verry good bargain from him

Sworn to and Subscribed this 19th day of July 1823
before us

| Saml. Perrin | JP | (Seal) | William Rainey |
| Patrick Gibson | JP | (Seal) | James Lard |

Stokes County

****

Robert W. Mosby & Others Vs. George Brooks [1821]
Civil Actions
Stokes County, Nc

Robert W. Mosby
& wife & others
Vs
George Brooks
Bill in Equity
Stokes County
filed Apl 1821

To the Honorable the Judge of the Court of Equity for Stokes County

The Bill of Complaint of R.W. Mosby & his Wife Jane Mosby, & James L. Mosby, William L. Mosby & Robert G. Mosby, which them last mamed persons are infants under the age of 21 years respectively & **[Faded]** in this behalf by their next friend R.W. Mosby - lawful **[Faded]**
against
George Brooks, Defendant

Humbly Complaining shew unto your Honor your Orators R.W. Mosby of Stokes County & his Wife Jane Mosby, James L. Mosby, William L. Mosby & Robert G. Mosby, all of Stokes County, that your Orator & Oratrix R.W. Mosby & Jane intermarried with each other in the State of Virginia on the 8th day of October A.D 1812 or thereabouts, where they then resided; & that the said Jane is the daughter of one Chancellor H Saunders of Powhatan County in Virginia who after the said intermarriage, gave to his said daughter Jane by way of advancement a certain negro slave by the name of Cloe & her child John, during her natural life as the seperate Estate of the said Jane, exclusive of the claim or control of her said husband or any other person, with remainder to the Child or all the children of the said Jane; and that the said Chancellor made & duly executed a deed of Conveyance to the said Jane for the said slaves, bearing date the 20th day of January A.D. 1818 or there abouts, in

Stokes County

& by which he conveyed & [?] the said slaves in the form & manner aforesaid which said Deed was duly proved & recorded according to the laws of Virginia in the Court of Powhatan County & said State, where all the said parties there resided - Your Orator & Oratrix further shew, that your Orator R.W. Mosby removed to Stokes County about the month of November A.D. 1818 & hath continued to reside there with his family since that time: Your Orators & Oratrix further shew that your Orators James L Mosby, William L Mosby & Robert G Mosby are the children of the said Jane & that said James & William were born at the time of making the said Deed of Conveyance & the said Robert G hath been born since the said Deed was made and that they are advised, that under & by virtue of the said Deed (a Copy whereof is hereunto annexed as a part of this Bill of Complaint) The said Jane is entitled to all the said slaves that [Faded] during her life to her seperate use & as her seperate & exclusive Estate, not subject to the debts, control or disposition of her said Husband Robert W Mosby or any after taken husband & that your Orators James, William, & Robert and any after born Children and will be intitled to the same [?] remainder -- it is also shewn to your Honor, that your Orator Robert W Mosby became indebted to one William Barr of Stokes in a small sum of Money not exceeding one hundred Dollars & that said Barr obtained Judgments therefor against your said Orator before a Justice of the Peace & sent out Executions & placed them in the hands of one Milton Campbell a Constable, who levied on the said Cloe & a small Child of hers called Brittania & advertised them for sale to satisfy the said Executions: That your Orator Robert W. well knowing that said slaves were not liable to be sold for his debts & at the same time, not wishing that any person should be deceived & purchase the same as his property made it generally known how the said slaves were conveyed & came also to an agreement with the said Barr through his agent that the said slaves should not then be sold under the said Executions; & the said Barr wrote to that effect to the said Campbell; and your Orator Robert W did not in consequence thereof attend on the day appointed for the sale & the said Campbell, not regarding the directions of the plaintiff offered the said slave Cloe & her small child called Brittania for sale under the said Executions on the [Blank] day of November 1820 or there abouts at Stokes County, where one George Brooks of said County became the purchaser thereof at & for the price of One hundred & Seventy five dollars & twenty five cents or there abouts & took the said two slaves into his

Stokes County

possession -- and it is further shewn that it was well known to the said George that the said Slaves were the separate property of your Oratrix Jane & her Children & that the said George, on the day of the sale, in order to purchase them at a very low rate, mentioned several times to the bye-standers that the property of said slaves was on [?] & thereby prevented sundry persons from bidding for them. And it is also shewn that the said George threatens to remove the said Slaves out of the limits of this State and beyond the jurisdiction of this Honorable Court, with the [?] of defeating the rights pf your Oratrix Jane & her said children, under the pretence that the same are the property of your Orator Robert W Mosby & are liable to his debts: Whereas your Orator & Oratrix Robert W Mosby & Jane, on behalf & in right of the said Jane Exclusively & your Orator James, William & Robert Ch[?], that they are advised that the said Gift from C.H. Saunders to the said Jane & her children is valid in this Court, notwithstanding the same was not made to a Trustee for the use of said Jane & that this Honorable Court will protect the right of said Jane to the said Slaves as her separate Estate: And your Orators & Oratrix further shew that the said George Brooks hath been required on behalf of your Oratrix Jane & your Orators James, William & Robert G not to remove the said slaves, as he has threatened & also to [Faded] them for their use, as in Equity as he ought: But now so it is brought [Faded] your Honor that said George still holds the said slaves & refuses to deliver up the same: All which is con[Faded] to Equity & trust to the injury of your Oratrix Jane & her said children: In [?] consideration whereof & because your said Orators & oratrix are without remedy [Faded] in this Court: And to the End that the said George Brooks may on his Corporal Oath full true & perfect answers make full & singular the premises & that he may be restrained from removing the said slaves without the State & be compelled to produce the same according to such decree & order as this Honorable Court may make & also that the said slaves may be deemed & held to be the Separate property of the said Jane & her children & that the said George them at law in trust for them & that he may be compelled to carry them to some descent person to be appointed by your Honor as a Trustee for your Oratrix & her said children according to the true intent & meaning of the said deed & Conveyance made by the said Chancellor H Saunders & that your said Oratrix & her said children may have such other relief as their case may require: May it please your Honor to grant to your Orators & Oratrix a writ to be directed to the Sheriff of Stokes

Stokes County

County commanding him to take into his Custody the said two slaves & them to keep subject to the further Order of the Court, until the said George **[Rest of line faded]**.
shall enter into bond with good security in such sum as Your Honor may direct, with Condition that he will produce said Slaves & perform such **[?]** as Your Honor may from time to time make in the premises do**[Torn]** grant the States Writ of Subpoena to be directed to **[Torn]** said George commanding him to be & appear at the **[Faded]** time of this Honorable Court to be held on & at, & then & there to answer & according to the co**[Faded]** Court -- and your Orator & Oratrix will ever pray &c.
Thomas Ruffin

North Carolina
Robert W Mosby maketh oath that the several matters of fact set forth in the foregoing Bill of Complaint as of his own knowledge are true & the rest he believes to be true: And that the said Slaves Cloe & Brittania are of the value of seven hundred dollars in his belief
Robt. W Mosby
Sworn to before me at Orange County the 29th Novemr. 1820
T Nash JSCLE

The Clerk & Mastre of the Court of Equity for Stokes County will issue a copy of the within Bill of Subpoena and also a Writ directed to the Sheriff of said County commanding him to take into his possn. the said Negroes Cloe & Brittannia & them so to keep until the further order of the Court of Equity of said County **[Faded]** the said George Brooks shall enter into Bond with good Security double the values of said negros that they shall be forthcoming to answer such order & decree as shall be made in the premises -- the Complainants giving Bond & Security according to Law
T Nash JSC LE

Copy of a deed
CH Saunders to Jane Mosby
Powhatan County
James L Mosby, Wm L Mosby, Robt G Mosby

(Copy of Deed refered to in the Writ of Complaint)

Stokes County

This Indenture made the 2oth Jany. in the year 1818 Between Chancellor H Saunders on the one part and his daughter Jane Mosby of the other part; Witnesseth that the said Chancellor hath bargained, sold, and conveyed and by these presents doth bargain sell and convey to the said Jane a negro woman named Cloe with her child John[?] together with all future increase of the said Cloe to have and possess the said Negroes, during her natural life, to her separate and sole use, exclusive of the claim or title of her husband and all other persons remainder to the child or all Children of the said Jane and upon the death of either or any of the said children under twenty one years of age being unmarried and without issue remainder to the survivor or survivors of them; and upon the death of all the said children being unmarried, and under twenty one, with[?] the remainder to the heirs general of the said Jane **[Torn]** and the said C.H. Saunders doth warrant spe**[Torn]** the title hereby conveyed and hath signed & sealed this indenture the day and year aforesaid. Witness.

C.H. Saunders

Frans. Watkins, Jos. Stovall, Jos. W. Ayres, R.J. Woodson.

****

Joel Dickerson Vs. Phillip Fogler [1811]
Civil Action
Stokes County, NC

State of North Carolina
Stokes County

To Joseph Brown, and William Stroud Esquires, of the County of Clarke & State of Georgia, Greeting: We reposing especial trust and confidence in your integrity, Do authorise and empower you to cause Aaron Woodward, Jonathan Milton, John Chishum & Thomas Tramel to appear before you, at such time and place as you may appoint, and them on oath to examine touching all such matters and things as they shall know of concerning a certain matter of controversy in our Court of Pleas and Quarter Sessions, for the County of Stokes pending, wherein Joel Dickerson is plaintiff, and Philip Fogler defendant. And these depositions in writing by you so taken, the same to transmit, seales with your seals, to our Court to be held for the said

Stokes County

County, on the 2nd Monday of March next, to be read in evidence in behalf of the said Joel Dickerson in said controversy.
Witness; Robt. Williams Clerk of our said Court, the second Monday of December 1811   Rob. Williams CC

Georgia   }
Clarke County }

Pursuant to the annexed Commission to us directed, from the Honorable the Court of Pleas and Quarter Sessions in the County of Stokes and State of North Carolina under the Signature of Robert Williams the Clerk thereof, at the House of Major Joseph Brown in the Town of Watkinsville in the County and State first aforesaid on the Seventh day of february eighteen hundred and twelve, between the Hours of ten in the forenoon and four in the afternoon of that day, Joel Dickerson only being we proceeded to take the following Depositions of Aaron Woodward, Jonathan Melton Thomas Trammel and John Chisholm of lawful age, who having beeb first sworn upon the Holy Evangelist of Almighty God to depose the truth the whole truth and nothing but the truth between the said Parties named in the said Commission depose and say as follows, First,

      Aaron Woodward, deposeth and saith that he was present in the Month of February in the Year eighteen hundred and four, in the City of Charleston South Carolina, when Joel Dickerson of the County of Clarke & State of Georgia, purchased from on board a Ship Commanded by a Capt. Williams and said to belong toTann**[Faded]** & Cox of the said City for the sum of Three Hundred and thirty Dollars an African Negro boy named Dick aged about fourteen or fifteen Years; That this Deponent assisted in Counting the Money paid by the said Joel for the said Negro, and then saw the said Negro delivered by the Seller or his Agent to the said Joel, that the said Joel brought the said Negro to his home in the County of Clarke aforesaid, that the Deponent accompanied the said Joel home & hath frequently since that time and the beginning of the Year eighteen hundred and eleven, seen the said Negro in the possession of the said Joel who always claimed & used him as his own -- That this Deponent lodged at the House of the said Joel the night when the said Negro Dick was taken away or absconded from the Plantation of the said

Stokes County

Joel; that this Deponent accompanied the said Joel at his request to the County of Stokes North Carolina in the Month of July last for the purpose of identifying the said Negro Dick, That he saw the said Negro Dick who had been previously found by the said Joel in the possession of one Phillip Fogler in the County of Stokes North Carolina, and immediately knew the said negro to be the same negro so purchased by the said Joel in Charleston as aforesaid; That **[Smudged]** (Towit about the latter End of July) he the said Joel demanded the said Negro as his the said Joel's right of the said Fogler, who then and there refused to deliver the said Negro to the said Joel -- That this Deponent Conceives that the said Negro was and is of the value of five hundred Dollars -- That the said Negro Dick had Marks on the face and breast which African Negroes usually have, and was rather strongly made.

Aaron Woodward

    Jonathan Melton deposeth and Saith that he was and is well acquainted with a Negro Man Slave named Dick, and he knew him to be the property of and in possession of Joel Dickerson of Clarke County Georgia for five or six years past; that the said Negro had African Marks on his temples and forehead and was rather stoutly built and well Made and is now, as he supposes, of the age of twenty to twenty four years, and had the Character of being a very honest and valuable Slave and was and is as this Deponent thinks, of the value of five Hundred Dollars at least; And this Deponent further saith that, in the Month of February eighteen hundred and eleven, the said Joel informed this Deponent that the said Negro Dick had then lately been Carried away or absconded from the Plantation of the said Joel in said County and applied to this Deponent to take a trip in search of the said Negro, that this Deponent rode several hundred Miles in Company with the said Joel's son for that purpose, and having got upon the track, they pursued until they lost the trace of the Course the said Negro had taken, That on his this Deponents return he informed the said Joel of the Circumstances of his ride, and of his having found some trace of the Course of the said Negro -- That the said Joel then pursued and on his return told this Deponent that he had found the said Negro in Stokes County North Carolina, and requested this Deponent to go to North Carolina for the purpose of proving the right of the said Joel to the said Negro, and this Deponent saith that he accompanied the said

Stokes County

Joel and saw the said Negro Dick in the possession of Philip Fogler in Stokes County North Carolina about the latter end of July last -- Thus this Deponent knows the said Negro he so saw in the possession of Fogler as aforesaid to be the same Negro he so long knew in the possession of the said Joel in Clarke County as aforesaid -- That the said Joel then and there towit in Stokes County as aforesaid demanded the said Negro of the said Fogler, who repeatedly refused to deliver the said Negro to the said Joel.

      his
Jonathan X Melton
      Mark

Thomas Trammel deposeth and saith that he was and is well acquainted with an African Negro Man slave named Dick as the property of and is the possession of Joel Dickerson of the County of Clarke, Georgia for six or seven years prior to the time when the said Negro was taken, or ran away, from the Plantation of the said Joel about the time of the Big Snow in January eighteen hundred and eleven, That the said Negro had some Marks on his Temples and face, and this Deponent supposes was about three or four and twenty years of age, and that he would weigh when in health about one hundred and fifty Pounds -- That the said Negro had a Wife at this Deponents house, which was in the Neighbourhood of the said Joel's farm; That the said Negro had a good Character, and was as valuable as Negroes of his age generally are.

                                                    Thomas Trammel

---

John Chisholm deposeth and saith that he knew a Certain African Negro Man Slave named Dick to be the property and in the possession of Joel Dickerson in the County of Clarke Georgia about six Years before the said Negro was Carried away, or left the Plantation of the said Joel about the time of the big Snow in the beginning of the Year eighteen hundred and eleven; That the said Negro bore an honest Character and was a valuable slave and well worth five hundred Dollars, and was as this Deponent thinks of about the Middle size, and appeared to be aged fourteen or fifteen Years when this Deponent first knew him -- And this Deponent further saith that his Plantation adjoins the Plantation of the said Joel whence this Deponent had very frequent opportunities of seeing the said Negro & knew him as well as if the said Negro had belonged to him.

Stokes County

Jno. Chisholm

Georgia }
Clarke County }

We the Subscribers two of the acting Justices of the Peace in and for the County and State aforesaid, and also Commissioners in the annexed Commission named, Do hereby Certify that Aaron Woodward, Jonathan Melton, Thomas Trammel and John Chisholm the Witnesses in the said Commission named were duly by us examined having been first duly sworn as aforesaid, at the time and place herein before mentioned and that the said Witnesses signed and acknowledged their respective examinations in our presence
Given under our hands & Seals at Watkinsville in the County and State aforesaid this 7th feb 1812
Jos Brown JP   (Seal)
Wm. StroudJP   (Seal)

****

Elisha Abbot Vs. William Hill [1819]
Civil Action
Stokes County, NC

Elisha Abbott Vs. William Hill
Dep. Po for Deft
To April Term 1819

State of North Carolina
To Dudley Glass & Peter Reavis
Esquires, of the County of Halifax Virginia Greeting:
    We reposing especial trust and confidence in your integrity, do authorise and empower you to cause Sandy McCraw, Matthew Miller, John Harper, Polly Harper, William H. Carr, George Reavis & Andrew Anderson to appear before you, at such time and place as you may appoint, and on their oath to examine touching all such matters and things as they shall know of, concerning a certain matter of controversy in our Superior Court of Law, for the County of Stokes pending, wherein

Stokes County

Elisha Abbott is Plaintiff, and William Hill Defendant. And these depositions in writing by you so taken, the same to transmit, sealed with your seals, to our Court to be held for the said County, on the 3d Monday after the 4th Monday of March next, to be read in evidence in behalf of William Hill in said controversy.
        Witness, Thomas Armstrong Clerk of our said Court, the 22d day of February 1819
Thos Armstrong Clk

Halifax County State of Virginia
Depositions of George Reaves of lawfull age taken before us in our said County on the third Day of April in the year Eighteen hundred & nineteen at the house of Capt. Dudly Glass in the County aforesaid which depositions is to Read as evidence in a Matter of controversy in the superior court of Law in the County of Stokes North Carolina, now pending where in Elisha Abbott is Plaintiff and William Hill is defendent who being Sworn deposeth & sayeth

That some time about three or four year ago this deponant was at Elisha Abbots and a conversation arose respecting a certain Negroe Girl Tisbey which was then as he understood by Elisha Abbott & his family in the possession of Wm. Hill of Stokes County No. Carolina and Polly Abbott appeared to be disatisfyed with her father for Letting the said Hill carry the said Girl away & further observed that She was afraid that the Girl would not be as well treated at the Said Hills - as she was at Andrew Andersons & wished the Girl was at home and Abbott Said to his daughter Polly if she wanted the Girl that She Polley, Might go after her.

Q. by the Plaintiff - did you Not understand by Elisha Abbotts family that the Said Girl which Wm. Hill had in possession was Polley Abbotts and to be Given up by Hill when ever called for
Ansr. - I understood by the family that the Said Girl was Polley Abbotts & that Hill was to Give her up when called for & further this deponant Saith not
The above duely Sworn to before us the day & date above written.
Dudley Glass   (Seal)
Peter Reves   (Seal)

Stokes County

Halifax County - State Virginia
Deposition of Andrew Anderson of Lawfull age taken before us in our Said County on the third day of April in the year Eighteen hundred & Nineteen at the house of Capt. Dudley Glass in the County aforesaid which deposition is to be Read as Evidence in a Matter of controversy in the Superior court of Law in the County of Stokes North Carolina Now Pending wherein Elisha Abbott is Plantiff and William Hill is defendand who being Sworn deposeth & Sayeth.

That some time in the year Eighteen hundred fourteen Elisha Abbott & William Hill came to his house after a Negroe Girl Named Tisbey, which Girl this deponant had in possession for Several years for her Bord & Cloathing and Abbott Said to this deponant as you are tired of Tisbey, I shall take her away & Let my Daughter Elizabeth Hill have her a while on the same terms that this deponant had her, untill Such time that his Daughter Polley Abbott wanted the said Girl - and the Said Hill took the Said Girl on the terms above Named - & the Said Abbott Stated that when ever he took Tisbey away from Hill he Abbott, would put another Negroe in her place

Qs. By the dfd. did you not understand that the Girl Tisbey was to be my property if there was not another Negroe put in her place
Ansr. I did Not understand that she was -- and further this deponant Sayeth Not

The above deposition duly Sworn to before us the day & date above Written
Dudley Glass   (Seal)
Peter Reves   (Seal)

State of Virginia -- Halifax County
Deposition of John Harper of Lawfull age taken before us in our Said County on the third day of April in the year 1819 at the house of Capt. Dudley Glass in the County aforesaid which is to be Read as Evidence in a Matter of Controversy in the Superior Court of Law in the County of Stokes, No. Carolina Now pending Wherein Elisha Abbott is Plantiff and

Stokes County

William Hill is Defendend who being Sworn on the holy evangelist of almighty God deposeth & Sayeth
That some time between two or three years a goe he John Harper heard Elisha Abbott Say that he Gave a Negroe Girl - Tisbey, to William Hill. This deponant then said to Abbott -- he thought that he had Given the Said Tisbey to his daughter Polley, Abbott Replyed, so he had but polly could have another

Question By the Plantiff - did you See the Negroe delivered to Wm. Hill or know any thing of her being delivered.
Ansr. - I did Not See her delivered Nor know Nothing of Hills having her in possession, & further Sayeth Not.

The above deposition duly Sworn to befor us the day & date above Written
Dudley Glass   (Seal)
Peter Reves   (Seal)

Halifax County State of Virginia
Deposition of Matthew Milner of Lawfull age taken before us in our Said County on the third day of April Eighteen hundred & Nineteen at the house Capt. Dudley Glass in the County aforesd. which deposition is to be Read as evidence in a Matter of controversy in the Superior of Law in the County of Stokes No. Carolina Now Pending Wherein Elisha Abbott is Plantiff & William Hill is defendant - Who being Sworn deposeth & Sayeth

That some time - four or five years ago he heard Elisha Abbott Say that he intended to Give his Daughter Elizabeth Hill two or three Negroes

Quest. by the defendand - did not Elisha Abbott tell you that his Daughter was going to be Married to a certain William Hill Some years ago
Ansr. - I did and Abbott Said if his daughter did Marry Hill he Intended to Give her two or three Negroes & further this deponant Sayeth Not

The above deposition duly Sworn to before us this day & date above written
Dudley Glass   (Seal)
Peter Reves   (Seal)

Stokes County

Deposition of Orphey Anderson of Lawfull age taken at the Dwelling house of Capt. Dudley Glass in the County of Halifax & State of Virginia on the thirtyeth day of July one Thousand Eight hundred & Nineteen -- which is to be Read as Evidence in a case Now Pending in the Superior Court of Stokes County No. Carolina wherein Elisha Abbott is Plantiff & Wm. Hill is defendand who being first Sworn deposeth and Sayeth.

That at the time Elisha Abbott came after Tisbey, he Abbott Stated to me that he understood that I was tired of her. I said to Mr. Abbott I was not a tired of Tisbey -- but Abbott Said he wanted her to lend to his daughter Elizabeth a while -- and this deponant then Said to Mr. Abbott that (Tisbey) was his property & he had a Right to do what he pleased with her

Qs. - the first by the plt. did not I deliver Tisbey to Wm. Hill at Your house.
Ansr. - You Abbott Set (Tisbey) up behind Hill on his horse and Abbott and Hill Rode off together & Tisbey Riding behind Hill on his Horse & further this deponant Sayeth Not   Orpha Anderson

The above deposition duly Sworn to before us in our said County the day & date written
Dudley Glass   (Seal)
Peter Reves   (Seal)

Deposition of Andrew Anderson of Lawfull age taken at the Dwelling house of Capt. Dudley Glass in the County of Halifax & State of Virginia on the thirtyeth day of July Eighteen hundred & Nineteen which is to be Read as Evidence in a case Now Pending in the Superior court of Stokes County No. Carolina wherein Elisha Abbott is Plantiff and William Hill is defendent who being first Sworn deposeth and Sayeth -- that five years ago last March Elisha Abbott & William Hill came to his house in Company (together) after a Negroe Girl (Tisbey) the property of Elisha Abbott which Girl had been at My house for Clothing & Victualing for Nearly five years -- and Abbott Said to this Deponant that he had come after (Tisbey) this deponant Said he would be Glad to Keep (Tisbey) longer, But Abbott Said as he had come after the Girl he should take her

Stokes County

away and let his Daughter Elizabeth have her a while on the same terms that this deponant her untill Such time as his daughter Polley Abbott Should Want her -- and William Hill then Observed that he (Hill) would be Glad to Get the Girl upon them terms.

Quest. - the frst by the defendt - did Not Elisha Abbott tell me to take (Tisbey) & keep her and if Polley Abbott Should want her in one Year, he Abbott would Give to me (Hill) one other in her place.
Ansr. - There was No set time Mentioned but Elisha Abbott Promised that if he Abbott took (Tisbey) away from you (Hill) he would Put one other in her place.
Quest. 2 by the Same - was (Tisbey) delivered to Me at Your house
Ansr. - Elisha Abbott Loaned you the Girl at My house on the Same Terms that I had her on and set the Girl on your horse behind you & you carried her from My house in company with Abbott.
Quest. 3 by the Same - did Not Elisha Abbott & Polley Abbott direct you to say, I Hill had (Tisbey) on the same terms that you had her on
Ansr. - they did Not
Andrew Anderson

The above deposition duly Sworn to before us
Dudley Glass   (Seal)
Peter Reves   (Seal)

Deposition of Polley Abbott of Lawful Age taken at the house of Capt. Dudley Glass on the thirtyeth day of July one thousand Eight hundred and Nineteen in the County of Halifax & State of Virginia who being first Sworn deposeth & Sayeth
That at the time William Hill and My Father Elisha Abbott brought (Tisbey) from Andrew Andersons to Fathers house, I was at home and William Hill Said to Me (Polley) I have Got Tisbey and your Father hath Loaned her to me - and I will Give her up at any time when called for

Quest. 1st by the Defd - did Not your Father State to me the same Morning I Started home from his house to take (Tisbey) & keep her, & if he did Not Give me (Chaney) within twelve Months That Tisbey was to be mine
Ansr. - if there was any Such conversation, I did Not hear it.

Stokes County

Quest. 2 by the Same - Was there No Set time when Tisbey was to be called for if calld for at all
Ansr. - there was Not that I know of
Quest. 3 by the Same - did Not Your Father offer to Give (Winney) Or a Small Negroe & one hundred dollars for (Tisbey) about Eighteen months after I had her in Possession if I would let him have her (Tisbey) again
Ansr. - If My Father ever Made you them offers I Never heard them - but before - Father Loaned you (Tisbey) he Profered to Give you Winney and you Refused to take her.
Quest. 4 by the Same - did Not you Claim (Tisbey) as your Property at the time of the Riot ay My house
Ansr. - I did Not Claim her as my Property Only in this way, I Told Father to take her along home if he ever intended her for me.
Quest. 5 by the Same - do Not you Expect that (Tisbey) will be Given to you if your Father Recovers her from Me
Ansr. - I leave that to the will of My Father.
Quest. 6 by the Same - did Not your Father offer to Give Me a little Negroe and one hundred dollars for Tisbey at different times after I had her in Possession if I would Give her up
Ansr. - if My Father ever Made you them offers I did Not hear them. But at the time of the Riott at your house Father offered to Give you a little Negroe and one hundred dollars - if you would go home with him & behave Yourself but you Refused the offer and Said that you would keep what you had and further this deponant Sayeth Not
Polley Abbot

The foregoing Deposition duly Sworn to before us in our Said County the day and date Above written
Dudley Glass   (Seal)
Peter Reves   (Seal)

****

Hugh Rose Vs. John Matlock [1823]
Civil Action
Stokes County, NC

State of Tennessee
Stuart County

Stokes County

In pursuance of a commission directed from the Superior Court of law for Stokes County in the State of North Carolina, authorising us to take the deposition of Robert S. Coleman to be read in evidence in a Suit pending in Said Court wherein Hugh Rose [?] with the will Annexed of Thomas Rose Decd. and John Matlock is the Defendant we have caused the said Robert S. Coleman to appear before us at the Court house in Dover, in the County of Stuart aforesaid & in the State of Tennessee on the fourth (4th) day of August 1823, and having duly Sworn the said Robert S. Coleman to speak the truth, the whole truth, & nothing but the truth, touching & concerning the said suit he deposeth and sayeth.

That he was the subscribing witness to the within Bill of sale marked B made by Philip Rose to Thomas Rose dated 23d. of February 1802 for three negroes, Wassar, Ben & Jerry & for other articles - that he was present when Philip Rose made the said Bill of sale and either saw him sign it or heard him acknowledge it when signed

That he is the subscribing witness to the within account marked A signed by Philip Rose & dated the 23d. of February 1802 & either saw Philip Rose sign it or heard him acknowledge it, and also a witness to the Credit given on the back of said account by Thomas Rose & that he either saw Thomas Rose sign his name to the Credit, or heard him acknowledge it.

Quest. - Was there any other subscribing witness to the Bill of Sale Marked B?
Ansr. - I have no recollection whether any other person was present or not at the time of signing the said Bill of Sale, nor do I recollect whether any other person was called on to witness the Bill of Sale or whether any person did witness it except myself.
Quest. - Was John Lilard present at the time of the execution of the Bill of Sale?
Ansr. - I have no recollection of his being present.
Quest. - Tell all you know about the circumstances which led to the getting of the Bill of Sale & to the Settling of the Account?
Ansr. - I lived a near neighbour to Philip & Thomas Rose for many years. It was said that Philip Rose was indebted to his brother and other persons & wished to pay his debts as he alledged and it was so understood on the

Stokes County

day of sale - I was at the Sale - a number of people arrended - and the property was offered for sale and most of it was purchased by Thomas Rose - One of the negroes sold was purchased Doctr Cox - The said Thomas Rose was said to be the largest Creditor - after the sale but whether on the same day or not I do not recollect, Thomas & Philip Rose settled & the paper which I witnessed herein enclosed marked B, contains their settlement - Philip Rose made the Bill of Sale Marked A to Thomas for the things purchased at the sale.

Quest. - How did the brothers live at the time of the sale?
Ansr. - they both lived at that time in the same house - Philip being a married man & Thomas a single man, at the house of Philip Rose - the brothers seemed to be verry friendly - the property remained about the house where they both lived after the sale and although Thomas was the owner, Philip had the use of it.

Quest. - had Philip any Credit in the neighbourhood after the sale?
Ansr. - he had not - after the sale he was believed to have no property - his neighbours all looked on him as insolvent & he was never trusted - On this account his brother Thomas was obliged to become his security whenever he wanted a Credit in the neighbourhood. I had an account against Philip Rose for Corn & other Articles & I kept it against Thomas & him both because Philip had no Credit - I believe the other neighbours kept their accounting in the same way - this continued to be the Case as long as I lived in the neighbourhood.

Quest. - How were those negroes regarded after the sale, that was purchased & conveyed in the Bill of Sale marked B?
Ansr. - I always believed & understood them to be the property of Thomas Rose, so long as I remained in the neighbourhood in the year 1817.

Quest. - Did you remain all night at Roses after the day of sale?
Ansr. - I do not recollect - but I think I did not for I lived within half a mile & seldom staid from home, within that distance and further the said Robert S. Coleman sayeth not.

Robert S. Coleman   (Seal)

State of Tennessee
Stuart County SS

    In pursuance of the enclosed commission we caused Robert S. Coleman to appear before us, two acting justices of the peace for Stuart County, on the fourth day of August 1823, at the Court house in the town

Stokes County

of Dover & County of Stuart - and the preceding deposition was taken by us and the said Robert S. Coleman was duly Sworn upon the holy evangelists of Almighty God - and the same was signed by the said Robert in our presence in his own hand writing and the said deposition was committed to writing at our request by C Johnson - In testimony whereof we have hereto set our hands & seals this 4th day of August 1823

Jas Gray JP   (Seal)
Joseph Smith JP   (Seal)

Stokes County

Chapter Three

Stokes County

Criminal Actions

North Carolina State Archives
Stokes County Records
Miscellaneous Slave Records
C.R.090.928.13

The State Vs. Celia (a Slave) [1852]
Criminal Action
Stokes County, NC

The State Vs Celia (a Slave)
Witness, Milly Gibson, $3.66
Clk   .20
                         $3.86

October 18th 1852
Receive payment in full
  his

Stokes County

J X H Gibson
Mark
Wm Bennett, No 52
```
           400
           366
           ———
            34
```

State of North Carolina }
Stokes County   }Fall Term, 185/

I, Samuel H. Taylor, Clerk of the Superior Court of Law for Stokes County, do hereby certify that at Oct Term, 185/ The Grand Jury returned a bill of Indictment the State against Celia (a Slave) which was a true bill and the same being duly entered of record, when a jury of good and lawful men being duly sworn and empannelled to try the issues joined in the case, who for their verdict do say we find the defendant not Guilty when Milly Gibson a witness for the State filed the annexed certificate of her attendance to the amount of $3 and 66 cents.
In testimony whereof I have subscribed my name.
Saml. H. Taylor C.S.C.

****

The State Vs. Silas (a Slave) [1852]
Criminal Action
Stokes County, NC

Witness, Jas. S. Hill $1.10
Clk   20
                        $1.30

Recvd. payment
Jas. S. Hill, No 86

State of North Carolina }
Stokes County   }April Term, 1852

I, Samuel H. Taylor, Clerk of the Superior Court of Law for Stokes County, do hereby certify that at April Term 1852 The Grand Jury returned a bill of Indictment the State against Silas (a Slave) which was a

Stokes County

true bill and the same being duly entered of record, when a jury of good and lawful men being sworn and empannelled to try the issues joined in the case, who for their verdict do say we find the defendant not Guilty when James S. Hill a witness for the State filed the annexed certificate of his attendance to the amount of $1 and 10 cents.
In testimony whereof I have subscribed my name.
Saml. H. Taylor C.S.C.

****

The State Vs. Bob (a Slave) [1851]
Criminal Action
Assault & Battery
Stokes County, NC

State Vs. Bob (a Slave)
Executed J.G. Hill Shff
by Thos M Puckett, DS
dismissed

State of North Carolina }
Stokes County }

To any lawful officer to Execute & return. Whereas, information has this day been made to me, John W. Bitting one of the Justices of said County on the oath of Prestly George Sr., that Bob a Slave on the 7th Inst. at the residence of said Prestly George in said county did Violently beat & bruise the said Prestly George with a club, against the peace and dignity of the State. This is therefore to command you to Arrest the Said Slave Bob and have him before some justice of said County to answer the aforesaid complaint and to be further dealt with according to law, herein fail not and have you then & there this Warrant. Given under my hand and Seal this 8th day of Novr. AD 1851.
J.W. Bitting JP

State of North Carolina }
Stokes County }

Stokes County

To the Keeper of the common Jail of said County Greetings Whereas Bob the herewith sent, you have been requested by Mr JW Bitting one of the Justices of the said County to enter into recognizance of the sum $50[?] with security in this said sum for his appearance at our next court of pleas & quarter Sessions to be held for the County of Stokes at the court house in Crawford on the 2nd Monday in Dec next to answer a charge of the State Against him and has failed so to do: you are therefore hereby Commanded to receive the said Bob into the common Jail of said County there to remain untill he be discharged according to law.
Given under my hand and seal this 8th day of Novr. AD 1851.
J.W. Bitting JP   (Seal)

****

State Vs. Negroe Peter [1806]
Criminal Action
Felony (Stealing)
Stokes County, NC

State Warrant against Negroe Peter
Constable Cost	4.0
Witnesses	6
taking to Gaol 3 miles	6.6
summoning & hiring guard	8
	£1.46

By G Shober

State of North Carolina }
Stokes County   }
John Clayton is hereby deputied as Constable for want of another.
    Whereas Information is made to me one of the justices of the Peace By Huriah Tate of Orange County, that a certain Negroe Man calling himself Peter did Steal & take away from Hillsboro in Orange County aforesaid One Sorrell Mare, the property of Jephania Tate of said County of the value of fifty Pounds which said Mare he the said Huriah Tate found in the possession of John Clayton who chased the said Negroe while riding said Mare - all which the said Huriah Tate swears that he believes to be true.

Stokes County

These are therefore to command you to apprehend said Negroe if in your County & him bring before me or some Justice of the peace for said County to be Dealt with as the Law directs. Given under my hand & Seal November 18th 1806
G Shober   (Seal)

Summons Huriah Tate, Andrew Moore, & Joshua Boner, Witnesses for the State.

Huriah Tate & John Clayton acknowledged themselves indebted to the State of N.C. in the Sum of fifty Pounds each - to be levied agt. Condition to be void if they make their personal appearance at next Stokes Court on the first Monday of Dec next, to give Evidence in behalf of the State or Negroe Peter, & thence not depart without leave
Done before Me   Uriah Tate
Nov 19th 1806   John Clayton
G. Shober

State of North Carolina   }To the Sheriff & Gaoler
Stokes County   }of Stokes County

You are hereby requested to receive Peter the Negroe, & keep him safe in the Gaol of said County, until he is discharged by due process of Law, he being accused of stealing a Mare & for so doing [?] [?] thereby
Nov. 20th 1806   G: Shober JP

Stokes County Nov. 19th
North Carolina
    Peter the Negroe confessed that he belonged to John Hunt of Orange County on Flat River that he ran away from his Master abt. the 20th of October, that he staid some time about Mr Canes & Terrentines quarter, & whose Negroes fed him, that John Perry a read haired fellow enticed him to run away, promosing to bring him safe, that he met said Perry on the road the other side of Hillsboro, that Perry gave him his Horse to ride thro Town, that he told him that he would overtake him at Mabanis, and some distance this side he overtook him & both staid all

Stokes County

night at Gilbreaths, where Perry ordered him as his Servant after they both had crossed the River, Perry gave him the Mare to ride, an both travelled together til this side Guilford C.H. where Perry left him, and gave him directions to change his Name & come to Salem, where he would overtake him. The said Negroe Peter confessed further that he had owned said Mare to be his own, and offered to trade her on the road this side Guilford, the said Perry also gave him Saddle & bridle & a great Coat, & promised to take him to a State where Negroes are free.

Huriah Tate swears that the mare now in John Clayton's possession was his brother Zephaniah's Property & stolen from him the last day of October & the Negroe confessed that that mare was the mare he rode.
Given before me a Justice of Peace for sd County
G Shober (Seal)

****

State Vs. Sam (a Slave) [1821]
Criminal Action
Communicating a Threat
Stokes County, NC

State Vs. Sam (a Slave)
Executed, N Moody
Const Cost	1.40
To 2 recgn	.40
To dismissing	.75
	2.55
	1.40
	1.15

State of North Carolina }to the Sheriff or any other lawful
Stokes County }to execute and return

    Whereas Constantine L. Banner hath this day made Complaint upon oath before me Thomas T. Armstrong an acting Justice of the peace in and for said County, that he is afraid that Sam, a negro Slave the property of Joseph Bolejack of the County aforesaid, will do him or his family some secret personal injury, or that he the said Sam will injure his

Stokes County

the said C.L. Banner's property secretly, and therefore he craves that the said Sam be bound to security for his good behaviour.

    These are therefore to Command you to take and apprehend the said Sam if to be found in your County and bring him forthwith before me or some other Justice of the peace for said County for his good behaviour, and he be further dealt with as the Law directs. Given under my hand and seal this 23d. day of February 1821.

                                        Thos. Armstrong JP
Summon for State, Nelson, Patrick & Maria
For Deft. Abel & Lucy

23d. February 1821, The within Warrant being returned before me, and the charge examined into it is ordered and adjudged that the Sam the defendant find security for his good behaviour and appearance at March Court and that the security enter into recognizance in the sum of five hundred dollars accordingly - judgt. against Joseph Bolejack the owner of Sam for $40 Cost

---

23d. Feby 1821, To Nathaniel Moody one of the Constables of Stokes County, The defendant Sam failing to find security for his good behaviour generally, and especially towards Constantine Banner, and for his appearance at our next Court of pleas & quarter Sessions to be held for Stokes County on the second Monday in March next, you are therefore commanded to Convey the said Sam to the Common jail of said County, forthwith, and you the keeper of said Jail are hereby Commanded and required to receive the said Sam into your Custody & keeping him there safely keep untill he find such security, or until he is otherwise discharged according to law. Given under my hand.
W:N: Gibson JP

We the undersigned acknowledge ourselves indebted to the State of North Carolina, in the sum of five hundred dollars, to be void if the within mentioned Sam comply with the requisition of the accompanying judgments.   W.N. Gibson JP
Joseph Bolejack & Samuel Bolejack

Stokes County

Chapter Four

Stokes County

Petition Exparte

North Carolina State Archives
Stokes County Records
Miscellaneous Slave Records
C.R.090.928.13

Petition Exparte

J.M. Covington adm.
Exparte
Decree
To sell slaves
To Sept 1852

J.M. Covington admr.   } June Term 1852
Exparte   } Petition to sell Slaves

This case coming on to be read upon the petition exhibits filed, proofs &c. It is declared by the Court that a sale of the slaves mentioned

Stokes County

in the petition is necessary for a Just & proper distribution thereof. it is therefore ordered & decreed that the petitioner James M. Covingtonsell said slaves at public auction upon a credit of nine months at such places in Stokes County as he may deem best, first advertising the time & place of sale for at least twenty days at the Court House in Crawford & at least four other public places in Stokes County, that he take bonds of purchasers with good & sufficient security & make report to the next term of this Court

Copy Test   M Hill CC
Slaves
Judith aged 25 or 30, Floyd about nineteen, & Will 12 or 14 years

****

Petition Exparte

Miles Foy & Wife et al
Exparte
Petition to Divide Slaves
To March T. 1860, Decree Filed

State of North Carolina   }Court of pleas and quarter
Stokes County   }Sessions, March Term AD 1860

To the Worshipful Court now Sitting
The Petition of Miles Foy and his wife Selena F.J. Foy of full age, and Isaac H. Nelson, William F. Nelson, and John H. Nelson infants under the age of twenty one years who petition in this behalf by their next friend John Hill, respectfully represent that they are entitled as tenants in common to the following slaves, to wit: Sally, and her children Nathan, Rebecca, Mary, Anderson, Jo, Louisa, Alfred, and Cora, and Margaret and her children Cornelia and Anna, that they are desirous to have a division of the same, and that a division can be had without a sale of said Slaves. They further show that petitioners Miles Foy & wife Selena F.J. are entitled to one fourth part of said slaves, and that your infant petitioners are entitled, each of them to one fourth. They therefore pray your Worships to appoint three freeholders, unconnected with the parties by blood or affinity, and to order and direct that they, first being duly sworn, shall divide said slaves as nearly equal as possible, and allot to

Stokes County

each of your petitioners his or her share in severalty, and that they make report to the next term of this Court. and may it please your Worships to make all such other and further orders and decrees in the cause as its nature and circumstances shall or may require, and that they will ever pray &c.
Jno. F. Poindexter, Atto for petitioners.

Miles Foy & Wife & others }Court of pleas & quarter
Proceedings to divide slaves }Sept March term 1860

    This case coming on to be heard upon the petition the proofs in the case &c, it is declared by the Court that petitioners are entitled as tenants in common, to the slaves mentioned in the petition, and that their several rights are as therein set forth. It is also further declared that said slaves can be divided without a sale thereof, and that a division ought to be had as prayed for. It is therefore ordered, and decreed by the Court that John W. Chambers, Marshall T. Benton & James Rierson Senr. freeholders be and they are hereby appointed to make said division, and that, first being duly sworn, they divide said slaves as nearly equal as possible and allot to each of the petitioners his or her share thereof in severalty, and agreeably to their respective rights, and that under their hands and seals they make report to the next term of this Court.

Miles Foy &c, Exparte
Petition to divide slaves
To June 1860
J.W. Chambers, M.T. Benton, & James Rierson, Commissioners

Miles Foy &c, Exparte
Report, To June 1860

State of North Carolina }
Stokes County }

    In obedience to a decree of the Court of pleas and quarter sessions for Stokes County, at March Term 1860. we the undersigned Commissioners, appointed for that purpose, after being duly sworn,

Stokes County

proceeded to divide the slaves mentioned in the petition among the heirs or tenants in common as follows, to wit:

Lot no. 1, consisting of slaves, Sally, Nathan & Cora is valued at $2300.00; and is drawn by John H. Nelson which is tha amount of one share.

Lot no. 2, consisting of slaves Rebecca and Joseph is valued at $2200.00 and is drawn by Mr Miles Foy & is to receive from no 4, $100 to make this share equal.

Lot no 3, consisting of slaves Margaret, Cornelia, Anna & Anderson is valued at $2300.00 and is drawn by Isaac H. Nelson which is the amount of one share.

Lot no. 4, consisting of slaves Mary, Louisa & Alfred is valued at $2400.00 and is drawn by William F. Nelson & is to pay No. 2, $100.00 which makes this share equal.

All of which is respectfully submitted this 23rd April 1860
Jno. W. Chambers   (Seal)
Jos. Rierson   (Seal)
M. T. Benton   (Seal)

****

Petition Ex Parte

James T. Jordan & others
Ex Parte
Petition to Divide Slaves
Filed Spring Term 1859
Jas T Morehead[?] Sol.

State of North Carolina }
Superior Court of Law, Spring Term 1859

To the Honorable Judge of the Superior Court of Law for Stokes County.

Stokes County

The Petition of James T Jordan of full age and Edmund M Jordan under age, who petitions by his guardian Daniel J Jordan,

Humbly petitioning show unto your Honor, that in the year 1843 Martha Martin, Edmund L Martin & A M Seals, conveyed to John J Martin, certain slaves in trust to be held by him, for the use of your petitioners and their eldest brother, Seth A Jordan, with the provision that as each one of them Costuique Trust arrived at age his share should be set apart in severalty, that their brother Seth A Jordan arrived at full age in the year 1856, and his share or third part, has been duly assigned and set apart in severalty to him, under a decree of Stokes County Court, made at March Term 1857: leaving two thirds of the slaves in the hands of the trustee John J Martin - That your petitioner James T Jordan, arrived at full age on 6th of March 1859, who is anxious to have his part of said slaves assigned him in severalty: That the Slaves now in the hands of the Trustee are the following, Amelia, Abram, May, Martha, Scott, Elly, Julia, Eliza, Samuel, Pleasant, Dolly & Harry, twelve in number, that Mrs Martha Martin holds a life estate under the deed of Trust in the slave Henry, who is now advanced in life, and Mrs Martha Martin the Tenant for life is willing that your petitioner James T Jordan, should take him at present valuation [?] possession for life. They further show to your Honor, that your petitioner James T Jordan, is desirous to have his part, to wit, one half in value of said slaves, set apart in severalty to him, which cannot be done by the Trustee, and by the Terms of the Trust in consequence of the now age of your petitioner Edmund M Jordan, without the aid of this Honorable Court, where Trusts are properly executed, and partition of slaves held in common, made: To The End therefore, that your petitioner may be relieved in the premises - May it please your Honor to appoint three freeholders to make partition of said slaves between your petitioners James T Jordan, and Edmund M Jordan, and the part assigned and set apart to your petitioner James T Jordan, be surrendered to him and the other part, remain in the hands of the Trustee, until the arrival of full age of your petitioner Edmund M Jordan, and to grant all such other & further reliefs by the [?] of their [?] may require and as in duty bound, your petitioner will ever pray

April 19th 1859
James T Morehead
Sol for petitioners

Stokes County

James T Jordan   }Ex Parte
Edmund M Jordan   }Petition to divide slaves

    This Cause coming on to be heard upon the petition it is declared by the Court, that the petitioners are tenants in common in the slaves set forth in the petition and that James T Jordan has arrived at full age and [?] right, to call for partition:

    It is therefore ordered by the Court, that Robert Payne, Robert Wall, and William C. Moore be appointed Commissioners, to make partition of the slaves mentioned in the petition, and to assign and set apart, one half thereof in value, to each of the petitioners and report to the present Term of this Court.

James T Jordan & others
Report of Division of Slaves

James T Jordan   }In Stokes Superior Court of Law
& others   }Petition to Divide Slaves Spring Term 1859

    In obedience to an order of the Court made in the above case Spring Term 1859 - we the undersigned Commissioners, herein proceeded to make partition of the slaves mentioned in the petition, between James T Jordan and Edmund M Jordan:

Lot number 1 includes the following slaves -
1	Elly of the value of	$500:00
2	Henry	$300:00
3	Julia	1000:00
4	Eliz	700:00
5	Samuel	500:00
6	Pleasant	350:00
7	Dolly	<u>200:00</u>
		$3600:00

Lot No 2
1	Amelia of the value of	500:00
2	Abram	1000:00

Stokes County

3	Mary		700:00
4	Martha		500:00
5	Scott		1000:00
			3700:00
Aggregate			7300:00
1/2 to $3650:			

the allot assign and set a part to James T Jordan Lot No 1
of the value $3600:00
and that Lot No 2 pay   50:00
    $3650:00

the allot, and se apart lot No 2 to Edmund M Jordan of the
value of $3700:00
which Lot pays No   150:00
    $3650:00

All of which is respectfully submitted
April 20th 1859
    His
Robert X Payne   (Seal)
    Mark
Robert Wall
Wm. C. Moore

****

Petition Ex Parte

James G. Martin & others
Ex Parte
Petition to sell slaves
adm.
March Term 1860

State of North Carolina   }Court of pleas & quarter sessions
                                     }March Term 1860

         To the worshipful Justices of the court of pleas & quarter sessions for Stokes County

Stokes County

    The petition of James G Martin of free age and Gabriel H Tucker and Martha E Tucker, under age who petition by their Guardian Benjamin C Tucker;
    Humbly petitioning show unto your worships your petitioners James G Martin, Gabriel H Tucker, and Martha E Tucker, of the county of Stokes, that they are tenants in common in two slaves, Esther & her child Maria, Your petitioner James G Martin, is entitled to two fourths under the purchase from William S Rey and from James B Tucker, and each of your other petitioners Gabriel H Tucker and Martha E Tucker, is entitled to one fourth,
    They further show to your Worships that your petitioners Gabriel H Tucker and Martha E Tucker, are under the age of twenty one years, and that their father Benjamin C Tucker, has been duly appointed their Guardian by Stokes County Court; by where they petition.
    They further show, that said slaves cannot be divided, without a sale: May it therefore pray your Worships, to order and decree a sale of said slaves, upon such terms as may be most advisable, and that the money be divided among them according to their rights, and that all other and further reliefs be granted, which the nature of the case may require, and as in duty bound they will ever pray
March 14th 1860
[?] & Morehead, Attys

James G Martin & others } Decree March Term 1860
Ex Parte   }

This case coming on to be heard upon the petition it is ordered by the Court that Thomas Martin Esqr be & he is hereby appointed as Commissioner to make sale of the slaves Esther & Mariah in the petition mentioned; that he sell them at the Courthouse in Danbury on Tuesday of the next Superior Court of Law on a credit of six months taking bond & approved security for the purchase money & that he advertise the Terms & place of sale at the Court House in Danbury & three other public Places in the County of Stokes - Ordered that the Commissioner report to the next Term of this Court.

Stokes County

Report of Sale of Slaves
To June Term 1860

In obedience to a decree of the county court of Stokes made at March Term 1860 appointing one commissioner to sell two Slaves (to wit) Esther & Mariah as the property of James G Martin & others married in the petition after advertising them at the Court House Door in Danbury & three other public places in said County I proceeded to Sell the same at Danbury on the 17th day of April 1860 on a credit of Six months and James G Martin being the last & higher bidder at the sum of seventeen Hundred Dollars became the purchaser and entered into bond with good Security all of which is respectfully Submitted.
Thos. Martin   }Commissioner
June the 1st 1860

James G Martin & others
Ex Parte
at Sept Term 1860

James G Martin & Others } petition to sell slaves
Ex Parte   } Septr Term 1860

In this case the Commissioner Thomas Martin having filed his report & there being no exception thereto, it is ordered that the same be confirmed & that the Commissioner be allowed seventeen Dollars to be returned out of the fund.
    Ordered [?] that the Commissioner collect the purchase money & after returning the costs of this suit including the allowance aforesaid that he pay me half of the rest due to James G Martin & the other to Benjn. C Tucker as guardian for Gabriel H Tucker & Martha E Tucker his wards & take their receipts for the same & that this order be Sp[?] in the minutes.

****

Petition Ex Parte
[Partial]

Stokes County

Valuation of Negroes

No 1			No 3		
Abe		550	Synthia & Hanah		375
Jenny & Aaron		425	Jordan		275
Jennet		<u>125</u>	Wiley		250
		1100	Martha		<u>225</u>
No 2					1125
Daniel		450	No 4		
Eliza		350	Hanah & Raymond		300
Sterling		125	Susan		115
Mary		<u>225</u>	Manuel		**[Torn]**
		1150	Andy		**[Torn]**
					1050

We have valued negroes as above & classed them , Jan 2 1833
Wm Cox, J.L. Bettings, Reubin D. Golding & Joshua Banner.

Valuation of Negroes
Jan 2 1836
Year 1836

No 1		No 2	
Hanah & Raymond	500	Cynthia & Child Lucille	500
Susan	250	Hanah	200
Jordan	400	Wilie	450
Manual	<u>600</u>	Martha	<u>400</u>
Drawn by Ann	1750	N Talley	1550

No 3	
Jeney & Child Lewis	530
Andy	400
Jennett	300
Aaron	250
Stephen	<u>200</u>
Widow	1700

Stokes County

We have valued Negroes as above & classed them
Jany 2 1838
Wm Cox, J.L. Bitting, A. Bitting & Joshua Banner

Stokes County

Chapter Five

Stokes County

Mortgage of Slaves

North Carolina State Archives
Stokes County Records
Miscellaneous Slave Records
C.R.090.928.13

Mortgage of Slaves

B Forsyths Obligation

Memo. Jany 12th 1811
    Recd. of Mr. Jeremiah Gibson two hundred & Seventy dollars for which I have put my Negro Girl Sarah in his possession to work for the Interest of the Said two hundred & Seventy Dollars and which money I am to return to the Said J Gibson within three Months from the date hereof or the negro aforesaid is to be the property of the said Gibson for the sum aforesaid of two hundred dollars of the aforesaid Sum is to be paid in hard money Witness my hand & Seal the day above written
Cost, $270   Benjn Forsyth   (Seal)

Stokes County

Test
John Gibson Jurat

Stokes County June Term 1812
    The execution of this deed was duly proven in open Court by John Gibson & ordered to be registered
Robt. Williams CC

Stokes County Ss.
Registered in the registers Office, Book No. 5, Folio 423
test A Robinson P.R.

Benjamin Forsyth to Jeremiah Gibson
Bill of Sale

North Carolina Stokes County
Know all men by these presents that I Benjamin Forsyth of the town of Germanton & County & State aforesaid for & in consideration of the sum of sixteen hundred dollars to me in hand paid by Jeremiah Gibson of the town, county & State aforesaid the receipt whereof is hereby acknowledged to have been fully received by me the aforesaid Benjamin Forsythe. I, the aforesaid Benjamin Forsythe for, & on account of the aforesaid consideration of sixteen hundred dollars have this day bargained, sold & delivered to the aforesaid Jeremiah Gibson the following property, Viz, my house & lot with the improvements thereon whereon I now live, in the town aforesaid, together with the land adjoining which I bought of Jacob Salmons, to have & to hold to him the said Jeremiah Gibson, his heirs & assigns forever, also the following negro slaves, Viz, a negro Woman slave about twenty two years of age named Silvy, one negro Girl slave about fifteen years of age named Fanny, one negro boy slave about thirteen years of age named Charles & one negro man Slave about forty five years of age named Adair, all which negroes, together with their increase hereafter, & the aforesaid house & Cotts, with their improvements. I hereby bind myself, my heirs, executors or administrators to warrant & defend to the aforesaid Jeremiah Gibson his heirs or assigns, a good & lawful title in & to free & clear of the Claim or Claims, Molestation or hindrance of me the aforesaid Benjamin Forsythe, my heirs, executors, or administrators, or of the Claim or

Stokes County

Claims, Molestation or hindrance of any other person or persons whatsoever, provided nevertheless that if I the aforesaid Benjamin Forsythe, my heirs &c shall well & truly pay to the aforesaid Jeremiah Gibson, his heirs or assigns, the aforesaid sum of sixteen hundred dollars with Lawful interest from the first day of July next, until paid then the above obligation & sale of the aforesaid property to be void, Otherwise to remain in full force & effect, in witness whereof I have hereunto set my hand & seal this twenty second day June 1810
Benjn Forsyth   (Seal)
Andrew Bowman Jurat

Stokes County June Term 1812
The execution of this deed was duly proven in open Court by Andrew Bowman & ordered to be registered
Rob Williams CC

Stokes County Ss.
Registered in the registers Office, Book N0. 5, folio - 423
[?] A Robinson

To the Honourable the Judge of the Court of Equity for the County of Stokes
    Humbly complaining Sheweth
unto your Honour Your Orator Jeremiah Gibson of the County of Stokes, that Benjamin Forsythe of the County aforesaid being seized in fee of & truly [?] possessed of a certain messuage or lot of land in the County of Stokes & town of Germanton whereon he now lives together with the land adjoining; which he bought of Jacob Salmon and also being possessed of the following Negro Slaves (Viz) a negroe Woman Slave about twenty two years of age named Silvy, one Negroe Girl Slave about fifteen years of age named Franny, one Negroe boy Slave about thirteen years of age named Charles, & one Negroe man Slave about forty five years of age named Adain and your Orator further Sheweth that the said Benjamin Forsythe being so possessed and being in Debted to your Orator in the sum of Sixteen hundred dollars for Goods, Wares and merchandize sold & Delivered and for money but to the said Benjamin, and in Order to secure the payment thereof with interest at the rate Six per centum per annum he

Stokes County

proposed to convey to your Orator the above mentioned land and Negro Slaves - and your Orator having agreed to accept the same the said Benjamin Forsythe by indenture bearing date the 22d day of June 1810 and made between the said Benjamin and your Orator did in consideration of the Sum of Sixteen hundred dollars to due as aforesaid, sell convey and transfer to your Orator and his Heirs executors &c all the right title and interest which he the said Benjamin had to the said lands and Negroe Slaves together with all the increase of the Negroe Slaves in which said indenture thare is a proviso contained that if the said Benjamin Forsythe his executors Heirs or assigns shall well and truly pay to your Orator the said Sum of Sixteen hundred dollars with lawful interest from the first day of July 1810 that then the said indenture and Mortgage should be null and Void - And your Orator further Sheweth that the said Benjamin Forsythe being also possessed of a Negro Girl by the name of Sarah and wishing to borrow the sum of two hundred and Seventy dollars applied to your Orator for the purpose of Borrowing the same on the 12th day of July 1810 which was loaned by your orator to the said Benjamin and to secure the payment thereof together with the interrest thereon the said Benjamin executed a bill of Sale to your Orator for the said Negroe Girl Sarah in which bill of Sale he did agree that the said Negro Girl Sarah Should remain in the possession of your Orator for the interest of the said two hundred and Seventy dollars and he further agreed if the said two hundred and seventy dollars should not be paid within three months of the date of said bill of Sale (which [?] date on the 12th of July 1810) that then the Negro Girl Sarah was to be the property of Your Orator as reference being [?] the two instruments of writing above mentioned will more fully appear, which your Orator prays may be taken as Part of this his bill of complaint. Your Orator further Sheweth that there is now Justly due and owing to your Orator on the several Securities heretofore mentioned the sum of eighteen hundred and seventy dollars of the value of nine hundred and thirty five pounds, being the Principle which your Orator actually lent and advanced to the said Benjamin Forsythe at the time he executed the Said deeds of Mortgage aforesaid and also interrest on the said Sixteen hundred dollars to this time and your Orator hoped and expected that the said Benjamin Forsythe would have paid the same without trouble or Litigation and for that purpose your Orator hath frequently applied to the said Benjamin to pay the same --- But Now So it is may it please your Honours the said Benjamin Forsythe combining and confederating to and with divers

Stokes County

persons at present unknown to your Orator, but whose names when discovered your Orator prays may be made parties to this Bill of complaint with words to charge them, contriving how to injure and Defraud your Orator of his debt hath actually declined and refused to pay the same on any part thereof --- All Which Actings And Doings of the said Benjamin and his confederates are contrary to equity and good conscience and tend to the manifest wrong and injury of your Orator. In tender Consideration whereof and in as much as your Orator is remediless in a court of law in as much as a part of the property is removed (to wit) the said Negro boy Charles) out of this State by the said Benjamin and the property even the whole of it is not sufficient to discharge the Debt owing to your Orator - he therefore hath no relief save only in a court of equity -- To The End Therefore that the said Benjamin and the rest of his confederates when discovered may upon their corporal Oath full true direct and perfect answer make to all and singular the premises and that as fully as if the same were herein again repeated and be interogated thereto and that he may sett forth whether he was not possessed of the property mentioned in the two instruments of writing aforesaid and if he did not mortgage the same in the manner above stated to your Orator for the said sum of Sixteen hundred dollars with lawful interrest and also the further sum of two hundred and Seventy dollars - making in the whole eighteen hundred and Seventy dollars - And that the said Benjamin Forsythe may come to an amount with your Orator touching the Sum due to him on the said Securities and may be decreed to pay your Orator by a short day Such Sum as shall upon Such amount appear to be due and owing to your Orator for his principle interrest and costs or in default thereof that the said Mortgaged premises and Negro Slaves may be let up to be Sold by the proper officer of this honourable Court and that your Orator may be paid out of the money arrising from the Sale thereof the Sum appearing due to him for his principle interrest and costs - and the said Benjamin Forsythe may in such Case be absolutely foreclosed of and from, all and every manner of Equity of redemption of said morgaged premises, and every part and parcel thereof, and that your Orator may have all such other and further relief in the premises according to equity and good conscience and the nature and merits of his case as to your Honours may seem meet. May it therefore please your Honours to grant unto your Orator a writ or writs of Subpoena issuing out of this Honourable Court directed to the said Benjamin Forsythe thereby commanding him to appear at the next Superior Court for the County of Stokes on the third Monday after the

Stokes County

fourth Monday in September 1811 and under certain penalties therein is to be limited requiring him to appear and answer the above allegations and further to stand to and abide such order and Decree in the premises as to your Honour shall seem meet and as shall be agreeable to equity and good conscience and your Orator as in duty bound will ever pray.
Jo Wihan[?]
Atto for Complt

Stokes County

Chapter Six

Stokes County

Sales of Slaves

North Carolina State Archives
Stokes County Records
Miscellaneous Slave Records
C.R.090.928.13

Sales of Slaves

Jno Crittenden
to T.P. Guinn

Know all men by these presents that I John Crittenden of the County of Hallifax & State of Virginia, For and in Consideration of the Sum of Two thousand Dollars Money of the united States, Have Granted, Bargained Sold and Delivered unto Thornton Preston Guinn Six Negroe Slaves (to Witt) Patt a Negroe Woman **[Torn]** and her five Children, Viz Lucey, Jack, Charity, Aggy, & Alford And the Right and Title of all and Singular, the aforesaid slaves I the said John Crittenden Doth by these presents Oblige myself, my heirs executors and Administrators, to warrant

Stokes County

and forever Defend unto the said Thornton Preston Guinn his heirs and Assigns forever against the Claim, or Claims of all persons Whatever. In Witness Whereof, I hereunto set my hand and seal this twenty second day of Decr. AD 1802
Signed Sealed & Delivered
before us   Viz.   John Crittenden   (Seal)
A Robinson Jurat
David Dolton

****

Sales of Slaves

Elizabeth Williamson's Receipt

The within note was given to up to me to be delivered by my Father Ezekiel Frost, 9th C M E under an order of the Court of Equity this 12 [Faded] 1819
Jas B. Frost
Em [?]

Received September the 11th of Ezekiel Frost, eighty four dollars & twenty cents, in full payment for negro Jenny, as will appear by a note of hand, given by the said Ezekiel Frost to Greene Moore, to secure the overplus, of the price of the said negro Jenny, and filed by the said Greene Moore, in the Court of Equity, which will appear of record. Which payment I hereby acknowledge as ample satisfaction for the above mentioned note.
                her
Elizabeth   X Williamson
             mark
Test
Elisha Childress
William Childress Senor

****

State of North Carolina   } In Equity
Stokes County   } October Term 1830

Stokes County

Pursuant to a decree of the Honorable, the Judge of the Court of Equity held at Germanton for Stokes County at Apl. Term 1830. I have proceeded to sell the Negro boy Harry therein mentioned and having advertised the said boy for twenty days, I proceed to sell the same at Frost's Iron Works, on the fifth day of June 1830 when Ezekiel Frost being the last and highest bidder became the purchaser at the sum of $400, and executed his bond payable twelve months, after date, with James B. Frost security. All of which is respectfully submitted.
Albert Moore
It is ordered and adjudged by the Court, that the above report be confirmed, and that the said Albert Moore retain the bond mentioned therein in his own hands Subject to the future order of this Court, and that upon the payment of the said money that the said Albert Moore be directed to make title to the said negro Harry.

October term 1831
    Albert Moore comes to Court & informs his honour that he hath received from Ezekiel Frost the purchaser of negro Harry all the money due upon the bond of the said Ezekiel and James B. Frost given for the price of said negro and that he hath paid one moiety of the money to Jesse Childress whose receipt for the said **[Smudged]** exhibits to the Court and that he hath retained out of the money sufficient to pay the cost of the petition.
    Whereupon it is ordered & adjudged by the Court upon the matters by the former decree retained for further adjudication that Albert Moore deliver to the said Ezekiel Frost the bond aforesaid, and execute to him a deed of conveyance of the said negro Harry - And that Albert Moore be allowed the sum of **[Blank]** for his labour and travail in the premises; And that the cost of this petition be paid out of the said money.

****

Sales of Slaves
Delivery Bond

Wm. Hampton's

Stokes County

To a Delivery Bond To Charles Beazley Constable
Miss Anna Hickman, Security to the same
The 15th of Sept 1851 by Charles Beazley

Copy of Notice delivered to Miss Anna Hickman
The 27th of Nov 1851

State of North Carolina Stokes County Miss Anna Hickman you will please to hereby take notice that at our next Court of pleas and Quarter Sessions to be held for the County of Stokes at the Courthouse in Crawford on the 2d Monday of December Next I shall Move the Said Court to obtain Judgment on a Delivery bond executed to me by William W Hampton on the 15th day of September last for the sum of ninety nine dollars and you are Security to the Same for the delivery of a negro woman named Fanny at the Courthouse in Crawford on the 2d Monday in October last levied on as the property of William W Hampton at the instance of the Chairman of the County Court of Stokes given under my hand and Seal the 22d day of November AD 1851.
Charles Beazley, Constable.

State of North Carolina }
Stokes County }

Know all Men by these Presents, That we, Wm W Hampton and Anna Hickman are held and firmly bound unto Charles Beazley, Const. in the sum of ninety nine dollars current money of this State, to the true and faithful payment whereof, we bond ourselves, our heirs, executors, administrators and assigns, jointly and severally, firmly by these presents. Signed with our hands and sealed with our seals, this 15th day of September A.D. 185/

The Condition Of The Above Obligation Is Such, That whereas the said Charles Beazley Const., has levied an execution at the instance of the the Chairman of the County Court of Stokes on certain property of Wm W Hampton, consisting of one negro woman Fanny, and which said property, at the request of the said Wm. W Hampton, until the same shall be sold: Now therefore, if the said Wm W Hampton and Anna Hickman shall well and truly deliver the said property herein before enumerated, to

Stokes County

the said Charles Beazley by time for sale at the Court House door in Crawford on or before the 2d Monday of October 1851 without damage or further hindrance, then this obligation to be void - otherwise to remain in full force and effect.

Sealed and Delivered in presence of

    his   Wm. W. Hampton   (Seal)
James X Sa[?]   Anna Hikman   (Seal)
    mark

****

Sales of Slaves

Sale of a negro ordered

It appearing to the satisfaction of the Court that a runaway negro slave called Cr[?]asa hath been in jail for 12 months - that the same hath been duly advertised for 6 months & no owner having appeared to prove property - It is ordered by this Court that the Sheriff, after advertising and conforming with law proceed to sell said Slave and appropriate the purchase money as in such cases required by law.

****

Sales of Slaves

Wm. Rands Receipt for $1300.00, 1819

July 5th 1879 Received of W Bitting the sum of One hundred an one Dollars and forty two Cents it being in full of all demands which I have against said Bitting in consequence of a purchase of four Negroes, for which Negroes, said Bitting has paid me the sum of thirteen Hundred Dollars.
W Rand
Ms Hay[?]

Stokes County

Chapter Seven

Stokes County

Hiring of Slaves

North Carolina State Archives
Stokes County Records
Miscellaneous Slave Records
C.R.090.928.13

Hiring of Slaves

Hire of Negroes

Year 1827		1830	
Abe	72	Abe	72
Danl	60	Daniel	55
Lucy	25.25	Manuel	27
Hannah	21.56	Lucy	24
Manuel	18.25	Franky	11
Collen	25.25	Collen & Lewis	20
	222.25	Liza	8
			217

Stokes County

Year 1828		1831	
Abe	72	Daniel	55
Daniel	60	Manuel	27
Manuel	31.50	Dilcy	29
Hanah	24.50	Collen & Lewis	20
Collen	18.50	Franky	11
Lucy	18.50	Eliza	10
Lewis	13	Lucy	5
Liza	6		157
Franky	7		
	251.01		

		Rent of Land Town Fork place	
1829		1827	70
Abe	80	1828	55
Daniel	60	1829	42.50
Collen & Lewis	30	[?] Town were rented in farming & produce. Privat rates	
[Torn]	25	C Mor[?] to one [?]	40
Liza	8	H. Huffman	35
Franky	11	W Sullivan - Haggar	55
Hanah	3.50	one set of [?] stones	12
Manuel	31.56	Town & Lott - Betty	130.51
	249.00	rent of land about town worth say $.50 a year for 5 years $2.50	

****

Hiring of Negroes

Farmer Negroes - hired for 1845 as follows

Logan to H H Reeves	$20
NR Boyles - fees Jim & Ben	120
Ditto - Dicy	11

Ally was kept by the Widow Farmer at $24 per annum in part of the yearly sum Boyles was to pay under his contract

Assets $151

Stokes County

Hires in 1846 up to in July 1846 - only one availd any thing to the Estate & that was hired to Ro Hines - Widow hired Negroes	38.50
To be charged as Assets recevd. before the sale of	29.18
the negroes to Nancy R Boyles	218.86

Farmer's note August 1843	$12.33
Int to 1st Jany 1845, 1 year 5 months	9.52
Costs	115.04
Interest to 1st Jany 1845, 1 year	6.90
	243.79
Deduct this sum out of 1st payt to	75
the Widow under the Contract	168.79
Int to 1st Jany 1846	10.08
	178.87
Deduct this Sum out of 2nd payt under Contract	75
	103.87
Int 1 year	6.18
	110.05
Deduct for sum to be paid by Widow	75
	35.05
Int to Jany 1848	2.10
	37.15
1848 to be paid by Widow	37.15
	00.00

Widow agreed to stand in Boyles place as to paying Mrs Farmer, she having bought of Crews one moiety & at Sale of Admnrs the other moiety

	75
	37.15
	Assets 112.15

Administrators 1st Jany, 1847 paid Farmer	$57
1st Jany 1848 Crews paid	$75
deduct balance due of debt	37.15
bal of Crews payt to Widow Farmer	37.85
Widow Boyles in money	51
Ailcy hired to Mrs Farmer	24
Mrs Farmer entitled to	112.85
1849, 1st Jany Mrs Farmer entitled to Crews payt.	75

Stokes County

Ailcy	24
Cash from admrs for Nancy R Hughs	51
	150
1850, 13th Jany	
Mrs Farmer entitled to 1.50 + 5.41 =	155.41
payable [?] Crews payt.	75
Ailcy	24
cash from Admrs for Mrs Hughes	56.41
	$155.41
Widow owes admnr for these [?] as follows	
1st January 1847 - cash advanced	51
1st Jany 1848, 51-37.85 of the instalt recd of Crews	51
1st Jany 1849 - Crews paid $75 leaving Ailcy & Cash	51
1850 Cash advanced by Admnr	56
	$209.00
Deduct for this sum paid Banners toward these sums by Nancy R Boyles	
	130.69
	68.31

Stokes County

Chapter Eight

Stokes County

Weapons Permits

North Carolina State Archives
Stokes County Records
Miscellaneous Slave Records
C.R.090.928.13

Weapons Permits

S. Franklin

Ordered by Court that Stephen Franklin a Coulored man be permitted to carry a gun

****
D. Tilly's Boy to Carry a Gun

Ordered by the Court that permission be given to David Tilley that his Negro man Slave John Shull hunt and Kill Squirrels around his the Said Tilley's plantation for twelve months.

Stokes County

****

G. Shober's Bond

State of North Carolina }
Stokes County }

Know all men by these presents that we Gottlieb Shober & Emanl. Shober are held and firmly bound to Thos. T. Armstrong Chairman of the County Court of Said County in the Sum of One hundred Pounds current Money of said State to which Payment Well and Truly to be made We bind ourselves our heirs &c Sealed with our Seals & dated this 13th day of June 1829.

The Condition of the above Obligation is such that whereas the Said G. Shober has obtained leave for his Negro Man Slave named Enoch to hunt upon his own land and plantation With a Gun to Preserve his Stock or Kill Game for his family Now if the said Alave Enoch shall be of Good behaviour towards the Citizens of said County then the above Obligation to be Void otherwise to remain in full force and Virtue.

Signed Sealed & delivered }   G Shober   (Seal)
in presence of   }   Em Shober   (Seal)
C.L. Banner

Stokes County

Chapter Nine

Stokes County

Coroner's Records

**North Carolina State Archives
Stokes County Records
Miscellaneous Slave Records
C.R.090.928.13**

Coroner's Records
William M. Ziglar

Stokes County Dr.
To Wm Ziglar appointed Coroner
    To Services rendered in holding an inquest over the dead body of a negroe man Gabriel the property of Thomas James[Jarvis] in the fall of the year 1850 $5.60
to June 1852
Examined and approved
E.L. Martin, W.A. Mitchel & B.F. Willow - Comt. Finance

Stokes County

Chapter Ten

Stokes County

Miscellaneous Records

North Carolina State Archives
Stokes County Records
Miscellaneous Records
C.R.090.928.13

Miscellaneous Records

Exemptions

Ordered by Court that E L Martin be exempt from paying tax on Negro Mahali on her account of being Idiot, also on negro Clark on account of natural deformity for the year 1847 and every year thereafter

****
Permission to Sell Produce

I permit Lewis to sell his potatoes and peaches to any person see proper to buy

Stokes County

October the 10: 1830
Tandy Matthews

****
Permission to Sell Produce

Sept 19th, 1830 Phillis is permitted to sell Cucumbers and receive pay for those she sold before
M Blume

****
Hadly Reese - Affidavits

State of North Carolina }
Surry County }

Hadly Reece maketh oath that he lives a neighbour to Jacob Davis that he is well acquainted with him and he believes the said Davis to be nearly or quite clear of debt and that he believes him to be worth five hundred dollars of wheate his land and [?] is worth about that this affiant is a Merchant & would not hesitate to trust him to more than that amount
Sept. 9th 1831   Hadly Reese

Sworn to before me this 9th Septr 1831
S. Graves   C.M. E.

Surry County }
North Carolina }

This day Came Jonathan Kinshaw Before me WJ Haynes one of the Acting Justices of the Peace for Sd. County and Saith upon oath that he thinks Jacob Davis is worth four hundred Dollars or upwards
Sworn to and Subscribed Before me.
W J Haynes   JP   (Seal)

Stokes County

Surry County }
October 12th 1831 }

This Day Came Before me WJ Haynes one of the acting justices of the Peace for said County and Saith upon oath that he thinks that Jacob Davis is worth in property four hundred Dollars or upwards.
Sworn to Before me
WJ Haynes   JP   (Seal)

****

George Brooks Commitment for Sam
Dec 1836

Belews Creek, N.C., Decr. 6th, 1836
To the Joailor of Stokes County or Mr. John Vanhoy Esqr.

Dear Sir
    Please Receive the Negro boy Sam of Mr Rowlan Jourdan and confine him in your Joail untill Monday next, at which time I will be up and make arrangements With you & pay all expences for the Same and you will much oblige
Yours &c
Geo Brooks

****

When McKeal Fair[Fain] waz gon from home, his Negro went into his Mistress Bed and in her Room and that The Neighbours all Expected that her Child would be a Malato.

****

Stokes County N. Co.
John Hill 1840
Jos Betting

Stokes County

To food & clothing 5 negroes from the 5th July 1832 to last of April 1835 at $2.50 per month $412.50

To feeding bay mare from 5th July 1832 to the last of April 1833
$27.00

To Boarding John & Washington & sons from 28th Oct 1834 to the last of April 1835 $48.00

To feeding three head of horses the same time @ $4.00 per month each
$72.00

To keeping Colt from Oct 1834 to Aug 1835 @ $2.00 $20.00

To feeding 6 Negroes from 28th Oct 1834 to last of April 1835 at $2.50 Per month each $90.00

To Boarding himself & wife & her daughter from the 5th April 1835 to last of April 1835 $16.00

To Fodder and five fodder [?] $5.00

To [?] Shatten Corn 15 bs $3.75

[?] proved by his own oath $44.61

T [?] of Jack $5.00

To let of Plantation $30.00

Out of State $9.00

Yadkin County

Chapter Eleven

Yadkin County

Patrol Records

North Carolina State Archives
Yadkin County Records
Miscellaneous Records
C.R.106.928.2, Box #2

Patrol Records

Huntsville Dist.
Patrol Jan 1864
A Copy delivered to W.W. Long to notify the Patrols
S.T. Speer Shff

North Carolina }
Yadkin County }

Court of Pleas & Quarter Sessions Jany Term 1864.

Yadkin County

Orderede by the Court that P.V. Welfare, Thos. Williams, W.J. Dickson, B.F. Jones, A.L. Laugenour, WS Williams, SB Harding be appointed a Patrol for the Huntsville for one year.
Teste   T.S. Martin, Clk, By N.A. Pos[Torn]

****

Patrol Com.
Hamptonville Dist. for 1865

Patrol Committee, Hamptonsville District
AW Martin, John E. Gough & Isaac Long Senr.

****

J Williams, J.S. Jones, Patrick Jones, W.W. McBride, Nat. Kernbough, L. Sintz[?]

Patrol Com. for little Yadkin District
July Term, 1864, RC Poindexter, Chm.

Panther Creek NC
July 4th, 1864
WW Long Esqr.

Dr Sir
    As you are one of the Special Court I deem it necessary that some one should suggest to you the idea of having some Patrols appointed for this district. If there ever was a time it was needed it is now, & I hope you will attend to it.
    Dont make a mistake and appoint me for I have served my apprenticeship.
Yours Truly
Jos Williams

****

Yadkin County

LD Kelly, HC Wilson & C Royal, Patrol
A Copy delivered to L.D. Kelly, September 3rd, 1859
W.W. Long Shff
By E.C. Roughton D.S.

North Carolina }
Yadkin County }
Court of pleas and quarter Sessions, July Term 59
    Ordered by the Court that LD Kelly, HC Wilson & C Royal be appointed Patroll for Yadkinville district.
Attest
TS Martin, Clk
By W.A. Joyce, D.C.

****

Order
Jonesville Dist.

Ordered by the Court that A.N. Tomlin, H.G. Hampton, Jo. R. Naylor be appointed a committee in the Jonesville District to appoint Patrollers for said District July the 5th 1859
Jas A Dodge
Order Issued.

****

Ed Phillips, George Lynch, John K Carter & Arch Poindexter
Patrol, Baltimore Dist. for the Year 1860

North Carolina }
Yadkin County }

    Court of pleas & quarter Sessions Jany Term 1860.
Ordered by the Court that Ed Phillips, George Lynch, John K Carter & Archibald Poindexter be appointed patrol for the Baltimore district for the year 1860
TS Martin Clk

Yadkin County

By WA Joyce DC

****

Patrol
Knoles District for 1860
Executed W.W. Long Shff, By EC Roughton DS

North Carolina }
Yadkin County }

    Court of pleas & quarter Sessions Jany Term 1860
Ordered by the Court that Calvin Gross, S.S. Arnold and ED Smith be appointed patrol for Knoles District for the Year 1860
Issued 21 Jany 1860
TS Martin Clk
By W.A. Joyce DC

****

Patrol Comt. for Yadkinville Dist.

WA Joyce, LD Kelly & AH Thomson
WW Long Shff

****

Ordered by the Court that J Williams & Jas N Dodge be appointed a patrol committee for Deep Creek District, Issued
WW Long Shff

****

Ordered by the Court that Tyre Glen, Joseph Conrad & Isaac Jarratt be appointed a Patrol committee in Baltimore district

Ordered that they be appointed
J Conley Clk

Yadkin County

***

Jonesville Patrol Comt.
Entered, Issued

N Carolina }
Yadkin County } January Term 1858

Ordered by Court that AN Tomlin, John J. Woodruff & HG Hampton be appointed a Patrol Committee for the Jonesville District for one year.
Jo Williams, Issued
Handed to Com. by Clk

***

Alfred Long & others
Patrol Order, Yadkinville District
Executed by delivering a Copy of this Order to Mr Whitacer
Feb 8 1856, G Holcomb Shff

State of N. Carolina } Court of Pleas & quarter sessions
Yadkin County } Jany Term 1856

Ordered by the Court that Alfred Long, John Steelman, William Steelman & William Whitaker be appointed a Patrol Committee for the Yadkinville District.
Test   T.S. Martin Clerk
         by W.A. Joyce, D.C.

***

Entered

Ordered by the Court that P Hunt, L Lynch & WW Long be appointed a Patrole Committee for the Huntsville District for One Year Oct 1857

Jo Williams Chm.
Issued

Yadkin County

****

Entered

State of North Carolina   } Court of pleas & Quarter Sessions
Yadkin County   } April term 1856

    Ordered by the Court that Jas. N Dodge, Jo Williams & Thos J Adams be appointed a patrol Committee for the Deep Creek District for one year
·B.C. Myers Clk

****

Patrol Order
Issued & Entered

State of N Carolina   } Court of Pleas & Quarter Sessions
Yadkin County   } April term 1857

    Ordered by the Court that RM Pearson, Jo Williams & Jas N Dodge be appointed a Patrol Committee for one year for the Deep Creek District.
Thos Haynes Chm.

****

A Copy delivered to the County
23 of April 1852
W[?] Felts Shff
By WW Long DS

North Carolina   } Court of Pleas & Quarter Sessions
Yadkin County   } Apl Term 1852

    Ordered by the Court that John P Clingman, Thomas Long & Joseph Gray be appointed a Patroll Committee in the Huntsville District and that they enter upon the duties of Sd Committee forth with.

Yadkin County

Witness   TS Martin CCC

****

Patrole Order
Jonesville Dist. 1852

State of North Carolina   }Janry T - 1852
Yadkin County   }

Ordered by the Court that Hardin Lafffoon, Francis Wood & John Y. Casey be appointed patrolers in the Jonesville District for the year 1852.
J Conly Chm.

****

A Reece, BC Myers & A Ireland
Patrol Committee
To Oct 1858
A Coppy delivered, W.W. Long Shff by Pm Jones D. Shff

North Carolina   }Court of Pleas & quarter Sessions
Yadkin County   } Oct. Term 1858

Ordered by the Court that A Reece, B.C. Myers & A Ireland be appointed a patrol committee for Speer's district for one year.
Attest: TS Martin Clk
By WA Joyce D.C.

****

Hardin S. Laffoon & Others
Patrollers in the Jonesville Dist. 1853
A Copy delivered the 10th day of March AD 1852
Wilie Felts Shff By H.G. Hampton DS

North Carolina   }Court of Pleas & quarter Sessions
Yadkin County   } Jany Term 1852

Yadkin County

Ordered by the court that Hardin Laffoon, Francis Wood & John Caisey be appointed Patroll in the Jonesville District for the Year 1852.
Test T.S. Martin CCC

****

Isaac Long & Others
Patrol Order, Hampton District
Executed by delivering a copy of this order to Isaac Long February 1 1856
G. Holcomb Shff

State of N. Carolina }Court of Pleas & Quarter Sessions
Yadkin County } Jany Term 1856

Ordered by the Court that Isaac Long - at the bridge - Isaac Vestal, Jas. T. Johnson, Hardy Williams, James West and James S Hanes[?] be appointed a Patrol Committee for the Hamptonville District.
Test: T.S. Martin Clk by W.A. Joyce D.C.

****

Patroll Committee
Please issue their Notices forth with
JC

State of No Ca } Court of Pleas & Quarter Sessions
Yadkin County } Jany Term 1853

Ordered by the Court that Alfred Well[?]ten, Christian Reinhart Jr, & Eph. Hough be appointed a Pattrol Committee for the Hamptonville Dist. and that the Clerk notify them
J Conley Chm.

****

Patroll Committee

Yadkin County

State of North Carolina } Court of Pleas & Quarter Sessions
Yadkin County } Jany Term 1853

  Ordered by the Court that Wm Sale[?], Tho Patterson & James Garrat be appointed a Patrol Committee for the Bean Shoal District & that the Clerk Notify them
J Conley Chm.

****

Jno Steelman, Joseph Reavis & Alfred Long are appointed Patrol for the Yadkinville Dist for 1 year
April Term 1855
J Conley Chm.

****

  WW Long & Others, Patrol Committee, Huntsville District
    To April Term 1856, A Coppy delivered
      February the 8th 1856
    Geo Holcom Shff By H Carter DS

State of North Carolina } Court of Pleas & quarter Sessions
Yadkin County } Jan. Term 1856

  Ordered by the Court that WW Long, Joseph A Bitting and TS Martin be appointed a Patrol Committee for the Huntsville District.
Attest: T.S. Martin Clk
by WA Joyce DC

****

    Patroll Committee, Baltimore District

Jany Term Yadkin Court 1853
Ordered by the Court that John J Conrad, Tyre Glen be appointed a Patrol Committee for Baltimore district.
J Jarratt Chm.

Yadkin County

****

State of NC } Court of Pleas & Quarter Sessions
Yadkin County } Jany Term 1853

Ordered by the Court that Wm. L. Vanestor[?], Hy Kist, Jos [?], & Will O Rine be appointed Patroll Committee for the Dist of Jonesville for the Year insuing.
J Conley Chm.

****

State of NC } Court of Pleas & Quarter Sessions
Yadkin County } Jany Term 1853

Ordered by the Court that R.C. Puryear, W.W. Long & Joseph A Bitting be appointed Patroll Committee for the Huntsville Dist for the insuing Year
J Conley Chm.

****

W.T. Phillips & Others, Patrol Committee
Baltimore District, A copey delivered
Geo Holcom Shff By H Carter DS

State of N. Carolina } Court of Pleas & quarter Sessions
Yadkin County } July Term 1856

Ordered by the Court that W.T. Phillips, M.C. Williams and Isaac Brown be appointed a Patrol Committee for the Baltimore district.
Test   T.S. Martin Clk
                By W.A. Joyce DC

****

BC Myers & Others, Patrol Committee

Yadkin County

To April Term 1857
Executed a copy delivered to BC Myers June 15th 1857
G Holcomb Shff

State of North Carolina } Court of Pleas & Quarter Sessions
Yadkin County   } April Term 1856

      Ordered by the Court that B.C. Myers, Isaac Stinson and Albert Ireland be appointed a patrol committee for Speer's district for one year.
A True Copy
T.S. Martin, Clk By WA Joyce DC

****

J Williams & James R Dodge, Pat. Comt.
A Copy delivered, WW Long Shff

North Carolina } Court of Pleas & quarter Sessions
Yadkin County } Oct. Term 1858

      Ordered by the Court that Joseph Williams & James R Dodge be appointed a patrol Committee for the Deep Creek district for one Year.
Attest: T.S. Martin Clk
By Will A. Joyce

****

Entered

Edmund Wilburn, James Haynes & James West Appointed Patrollers in the Hamptonville Dist.
Issued

****

Issue an Order
J Williams
Issued

Yadkin County

Will the Court please Apoint LD Kelly & HC Wilson & C Royal Patrole for Yadkinville District.

****

Patrolers to be appointed
J Jarratt, Chm.

Patroles for Baltimore District: Edward Phillips, John W. Creson & Tyre Patterson.

Patrolers for Bean Shoal District: Wilie Shoars, Thomas W Davis & William Apperson son of Thomas.

****

Patrole Committee
Hamflins[?] Dist.

AW Martin, Josiah Conley**[Cowley],** John Hamflins, D.I. Fleming & I Olin Haynes
Entered

****

Hugh Carter, Isaac Williams & C.W. Williams
Patrol Committee, Copy Delivered to Isaac Williams
Septr. 1st 1852, Wilie Feltz Shff

North Carolina }
Yadkin County }July Term 1852

    Ordered by the Court That Hugh Carter, Isaac Williams & CW Williams be appointed a Patroll Committee for the Chinquepin and Deep Creek Districts.
T.S. Martin CCC

****

Yadkin County

Patrol Order

Patrol Committee for Deep Creek: Joseph Williams, CW Williams, Henry Snow[?], & Hugh Carter

In Huntsville Dist. RC Puryear, Jn L Williams & JA Bitting
Entered

****

Patrol for the County for 1860
Entered

Huntsville Dist
Benjamin Phillips, Thos. Williams, Giles Hutchens, Caleb Bohannon, Jo Williams, Nathan Hunt.

Baltimore Dist.
Ed. Philips, Geog. Lynch, Jno K Carter, Archibald Poindexter

Chinquepen Dist.
Sandy Hutchens, Joseph Steelman, Jackson Steelman, Wm. Steelman, Wm Gough

Yadkinville Dist.
L.D. Kelly, Russ Fulburt[?], H.C. Wilson, E.T. Hauser, R.O. Hare

Jonesville Dist.
L.L. Sugart, T.D. Hampton, CG Kent[?], Mathew Lindsey, Henery Marshal

Hamptonville Dist.
A.C. Cre[?], James West, Alphonse Dickenson, M.L. Martin, J.H. Ball

East Bend Dist.
Francis Digern[?], John Freeland, Wesley Shore, Samuel B Spears & Gilligut Martin

Yadkin County

Knoles District
Calvin Gross, Sherrill Arnold, E.D. Smith

Deep Creek Dist.
Wm Hall, John Cooley, Jordan Snow, Milton Campbell, FR Williams & Danl Zachary

Yadkin County

Chapter Twelve

Yadkin County

Sales Of Slaves

North Carolina State Archives
Yadkin County Records
Miscellaneous Records
C.R.106.928.2, Box #2

Sales of Slaves

September the 27 day 1856

philis - brout	} John Sheaks	$287
Calvin - Brout	} Ditto	$320

Sale of Jefferson - brout two Dollars $2.00

I doo hear Buy Certfy that the a bove is a Sail
Corect $609
Test Wm. S. Arnold
Allen Helton Executor

Yadkin County

Allen Helton Exec. Return
The Sale of these negroes is rising to Martha Vestal and her [?]
Paid 40

****

A bill of Sale from John Reece to
John E. Gough
State of North Carolina } June 6, 1859
County of Yadkin }
    Know all Men by these presents that I John Reece of the above named State and County, for and in Consideration of the Sum of Eight hundred and Fifty dollars, to me in hand paid by John E. Gough of the Said County and State (and the receipt of which Sum of Money is hereby acknowledged) have this day bargained, Sold, aliened and Confirmed and by these presents do bargain Sell alien and Confirm to the said John E. Gough his heirs and assigns one Slave a negro Girl named Temperance Caroline and aged about fourteen Years, and I hereby warrent the Said negro Slave Temperance Caroline to be Sound in mind and body and free from Constitutional diseases or defects.
    In Witness whereof I hereunto Set my Hand and Seal the day and date above Written.

Test   John Reece   (Seal)
Thomas A. Nicholson (Jurat)   Sarah Reece (Seal)
North Carolina }
Yadkin County }
    The Execution of the foregoing Bill of Sale was this April 2nd 1860, duly proven before me by the oath of Thomas A. Nicholson a Subscribing witness thereto.
Let it be registered.
TS Martin Clk
By WA Joyce DC

Yadkin County

Chapter Thirteen

Yadkin County

Petition Exparte

North Carolina State Archives
Yadkin County Records
Miscellaneous Records
C.R.106.928.2, Box #2

Petition Ex Parte
[Partial]

State of North Carolina } Court of Pleas & Quarter Sessions
Yadkin County } January Term AD 1858

    The Petition of C.W. Williams Guardian of William Beren, humbly praying, respectfully showeth unto your Worships, that he was appointed Guardian of his said Ward during the present Term of this Court, and that the debts due from his said Ward ammount to about fifteen hundred dollars, your Petitioner further showeth that his said Ward is possessed of one invided half in the following negro slaves towit Milly, Anderson, Alfred, Lucinda, Fanny, Bet & Handy, your Petitioner

Yadkin County

further sheweth, that his said Ward is possessed of a very small personal Estate beside the said undivided Half in the said Slaves, and that it will be necessary to sell the whole of the the said undivided half in the said Slaves, in order to pay off the said debts against his said Ward. Your Petitioner therefore prays your Worships to make an Order authorizing him to sell the said undivided half in the said Slaves upon such Terms as to your Worships shall seem just and reasonable, and that he may hold the proceeds of said sale for the payment of the said debts against his said Ward and the surplus, if any, for the benefit of his said Ward; and your Petitioner as in duty bound will ever pray &c
RG [?] atto for Pet.

C.W. Williams, maketh oath that the facts set forth in the foregoing petition are true, to the best of his knowledge and belief. Sworn to & subscribed before me this the 7th day of January AD 1858.
TS Martin Clk
By WA Joyce DC

State of North Carolina }
Yadkin County }
Court of Pleas & Quarter Sessions Jan Term AD 1858
CW Williams Guardian of William Beren
Exparte

This Case Coming on to be heard upon the petition, and the suggestion of Council, it is ordered, adjudged and decreed by the Court, that CW Williams guardian of William Beren, advertizing twenty days, at the Court house door in the town of Yadkinville, and at three other public places in the County of Yadkin expose to sale, to the highest bidder on a credit of six months, the said undivided half of the slaves aforesaid, taking good security for the purchase money, and make report to the next term of this Court

Appendix A

Appendix A

Glossary of Legal Terms

[Definitions of legal terms appearing in transcriptions within this book are derived from *Black's Law Dictionary*.

Agent: An individual authorized by another to act in place of another person.

Affiant: An individual who creates and subscribes an affidavit. Interchangeable with deponent.

Assault and Battery: The unlawful touching of another individual without excuse or justification.

Bailiwick: A given area over which a bailiff or sheriff has authority or jurisdiction.

Capias: A general name for different types of writs requiring and officer to detain someone in custody.

Certiori: A writ issued by a superior court to an inferior court for the purpose of an investigation into irregularities.

Commission: A warrant issued by a government empowering an individual to do certain acts.

Appendix A

Decree: In equity, a sentence or order of the court after considering the case.

Deposition: The testimony of an individual, taken under oath, through interrogatories. The testimony is usually intended to be used in civil or criminal cases.

Equity Courts: Courts that deliver justice according to the system of equity. Equity courts are sometimes called, "Courts of Chancery."

Esquire: A title given to sheriffs, justices of the peace, and barristers at law.

False Imprisonment: An individual who is placed in detention without his consent, and without lawful authority.

Fi Fa (Fieri Facias): A writ requiring a sheriff to satisfy a judgment levied from a debtors property.

Habeas Corpus: A writ commonly directed to a sheriff ordering him to deliver a prisoner, or an individual who is to be detained. The purpose is to test the legality of the detention, and not whether the individual is guilty or innocent.

Indenture: A contract by which bonds and debentures are issued stating the form of bond, maturity date, amount of issue, descriptions of assets, interest rates and various other terms.

Next Friend: An individual who acts for the benefit of an infant; or a person who is not able to look after his own business or interests.

Prima Facie: A fact supposedly to be true unless disproved by evidence to the contrary.

Subpoena: An order to appear at a specific place and time to testify upon a certain matter.

Appendix A

True Bill of Indictment: An endorsement issued by a grand jury upon finding sufficient evidence for a criminal charge.[4]

---

[4] Henry Campbell, M.A., Black's Law Dictionary, 6th ed. (St. Paul, Minn.: West Publishing Company, 1990.)

Table of Cases

Table of Cases

Civil & Criminal Actions

CASES

Elisha Abbot Vs. William Hill [1819]
  Civil Action
  Stokes County, NC--127

Hugh Rose Vs. John Matlock [1823]
  Civil Action
  Stokes County, NC--133

Isaac Evans Vs. John Odeneal [1822]
  Civil Action
  Stokes County, NC--110

Jemima Scott Vs. Lewis Williams & Others [1831]
  Civil Action
  Stokes County, NC--- 43

Jemima Scott Vs. Lewis Williams [1831]
  Civil Action
  Stokes County, NC--- 26

Table of Cases

Jesse Scott by His Next Friend Gemima Scott Vs. Lewis Williams
  Civil Action
    Stokes County, NC-- 30

Jesse Scott by his Next Friend J. Scott Vs. Lewis Williams [1831]
  Civil Action
    Stokes County, NC-- 14

Jesse Scott Vs. Lewis Williams [1830]
  Civil Action
    Stokes County, NC-- 17

Joel Dickerson Vs. Phillip Fogler [1811]
  Civil Action
    Stokes County, NC---123

Malvina Scott Vs. Lewis Williams [1831]
  Civil Action
    Stokes County, NC-- 22

Margaret Gittens Vs. George Hauser [1808]
  Civil Action
    Stokes County, NC-- 79

Robert W. Mosby & Others Vs. George Brooks [1821]
  Civil Action
    Stokes County, NC---119

Sally Scott by Her Next Friend J. Scott [1831]
  Civil Action
    Stokes County, NC-- 18

Sally Scott by Her Next Friend Jemima Scott [1831]
  Civil Action
    Stokes County, NC-- 31

State Vs. Negroe Peter [1806]
  Criminal Action

Table of Cases

Felony (Stealing)
Stokes County, NC---140

State Vs. Sam (a Slave) [1821]
Criminal Action
Communicating a Threat
Stokes County, NC---142

The Scotts Vs. Lewis Williams [1831]
Civil Action
Stokes County, NC-- 33

The State Vs. Bob (a Slave) [1851]
Criminal Action
Assault & Battery
Stokes County, NC---139

The State Vs. Celia (a Slave) [1852]
Criminal Action
Stokes County, NC---137

The State Vs. Silas (a Slave) [1852]
Criminal Action
Stokes County, NC---138

Index

Index

A

Abbot
  Elisha, 128
  Polly, 133
Abbott
  Elisha, 127, 128, 129, 130, 131, 132
  Elisha:, 132
  Polley, 129, 132
  Polly, 128, 132
Abbotts
  Elisha, 128
  Polly, 128
Adams
  James, 51
  Jas., JP, 51
  Thos J, 186
African Marks, 125
African Negroes, 125
Allen
  Rd., JP, 8
  Thomas, 63
Alley
  James, 9, 75
  Thomas, 9

Allin
  Richard, 6
Ally
  James, 68, 70
  Sal, a mulatto, 70
Anderson
  Andrew, 127, 128, 129, 131, 132
  Orpha, 131
  Orphey, 131
Apperson
  William, son of Thomas, 192
Armfield
  H.G., 1, 2
  Hance G., 2
Armstrong
  F.K., Deputy Sheriff, 15, 19
  FK, 29
  FK, Deputy Sheriff, 23, 25, 27
  Francis K., Deputy Sheriff, 15
  Francis K., Deputy Sheriff, 19, 23, 27

Hugh, 83, 86
Hugh, Esquire, 83
Mr., 68
T. T., Clk, 68
T.T., 58
T.T., Clerk, 31, 32, 36, 54
T.T., Clk, 38, 41
Tho T, 69
Tho T, Clk, 58, 61, 63
Tho. T., 55
Tho. T., Clk, 32, 34, 44, 48, 57, 62, 65
Thomas, 4, 128
Thomas T., 43, 45, 53, 142
Thomas T., Clerk, 36, 38, 39, 41, 42, 44, 46, 48, 51, 53, 55, 58, 69
Thomas T., Clk, 51
Thomas, Clerk, 30
Thos, 128
Thos, JP, 5
Thos. F., 3

207

Index

Thos. T., 174
Thos. T., Clk, 30, 31, 36, 39, 41, 42, 46
Thos., Clk, 51, 53
Thos., JP, 5, 143
TT, Clk, 73
ArmstrongThos., Clk, 51
Arnold
  S.S., 184
  Sherill, 194
  Wm. S., 195
Ayres
  Jos. W., 123

B

Badgett
  Abraham, 73
Bailey
  joseph, 37
  Joseph, 13, 31, 32, 33, 34, 35, 36, 37, 38, 39, 40, 45, 46, 47, 48, 49, 55, 58, 60, 62, 63, 64, 74
Baily
  Jos, 13
  Joseph, 8, 34
Ball
  J.H., 193
Banner
  C, 104
  C., 104
  C., Sheriff, 107, 108
  C.L., 143, 174
  C.L., Sheriff, 110
  Charles, 104

Charles, Sheriff, 107
CL, Sheriff, 117
Constantine, 143
Constantine L., 142
Jno, Deputy Sheriff, 110
Joshua, 154
Barnes
  Samuel, 51
Barr
  William, 120
Bayley
  Joseph, 67
Beazley
  Charles, 166, 167
  Charles Beazley, Constable, 166
Beldsoe
  Isaac, 90
Bennett
  Wm, 138
Benton
  M.T., 147, 148
  Marshall T., 147
Beren
  William, 197, 198
Betting
  Jos, 179
Bettings
  J.L., 154
Big Snow , Georgia, 1811, 126
Bitting
  A., 155
  J.L., 155
  J.W., JP, 139, 140
  JA, 193
  John W., 139

Joseph A, 189, 190
Mr JW, 140
W, 167
Bledsoe
  Isaac, 95
Bledsow
  Isaac, 90, 91, 94
Blume
  M, 178
Bohannon
  Caleb, 193
Bolejack
  Joseph, 142, 143
  Samuel, 144
Boner
  Joshua, 141
Bones
  Isaac, 102
Bonn
  Isaac, 107
Boones
  Isaac, 103
Bowman
  Andrew, 159
Boyden
  Mr., 68
Boyles
  Nancy R, 171
  Nancy R., 172
  NR, 170
  Widow, 171
Brooks
  Geo, 179
  George, 119, 120, 121, 122, 179
Brown
  Isaac, 190
  Jos., JP, 127
  Joseph, 123
  Major Joseph, 124
Bryson

Index

James, Agent, 91, 92, 93, 94, 96
James:, 85
Jas., Agent, 98
Js., Agent, 97
Mr., 94, 95
Squire, 91, 92
Brysons
  Squire, 91
Bunch
  Wm., 30
Burton
  John, 13, 33, 35, 37, 40, 47, 48, 49, 59, 63
Butner
  J., JP, 2
Buttner
  Adam, 107, 108

C

Caisey
  John, 188
Callaway
  Henry, 102
  J., 13
Callaways
  Henry, 100
Calloway
  James, 13
Campbell
  J, Clk, 25, 29
  J., Clk, 18, 22
  James, 7, 18
  James, Clerk, 22, 25, 29
  Jas, 7
  Milton, 194
  Milton, Constable, 120
Canes
  Mr, 141
Carr
  William H., 127
Carter
  H, Deputy Sheriff, 189, 190
  Hugh, 192, 193
  Jno K, 193
  John K, 183
Casey
  John Y., 187
Chambers
  J.W., 147
  Jno. W., 148
  John W., 147
Charter
  James, Jr., Attorney, 117
Childress
  Elisha, 164
  Jesse, 165
  William Senor, 164
Chisholm
  Jno., 127
  John, 124, 126, 127
Chishum
  John, 123
Christman
  Charles, JP, 95
Claughton
  George, 63
Clayton
  John, 140, 141, 142
Clingman
  John P, 186
Coe
  Isaiah, 68, 69, 71, 73, 98, 99
Cole
  Jn. C., JP, 71
  W.C., JP, 71
  William C., 69
Coleman
  Robert S., 134, 135, 136
Conley
  J, 184, 188, 189, 190
Conley[Cowley]
  Josiah, 192
Conly
  J, 187
Conrad
  Isaac, 3
  Isaac, JP, 4
  John J, 189
  Joseph, 184
Cooley
  John, 194
Covington
  J.M., 145
  James M., 146
Cox
  Isaiah, 8
  Wm., 154, 155
Crawley
  Thomas, 63, 64
Creeks
  Stewarts, 84
Creson
  Abraham, 9, 10, 69, 70, 71
  Abram, 74, 75, 76
  George, 71
  John W., 192
  Joshua, 71
Cresons
  Abram, 75
Cresson
  Mr., 8
Crews
  Mr., 171

Index

Crissman
  CS, JP, 97, 98
Crittenden
  Jno, 163
  John, 163, 164
Cumberland, 57

D

Dalton
  Jonathan, 107
Daniel
  Joseph J., Judge, 17, 21, 24, 28
Davis
  Ezra, 16, 19, 23, 27, 50
  F, 23
  J, 27
  Jacob, 50, 51, 178, 179
  Jas., 16, 19
  Mr. T., 8
  Saml L, 71
  Saml., 8
  Saml. L., 68
  Samuel L., 68, 69, 71
  Thomas W, 192
  William, 7, 50
  Wm., 14, 16, 19, 23, 27
Dickenson
  Alphonse, 193
Dickerson
  Joel, 123, 124, 125, 126
Dickson
  W.J., 182
Digern[?]
  Francis, 193
Diseases
  Billious Inflamatory, 116
  Cronie Disease, 116
  Scoffuers, 116
District of Columbia, 4
Dobbings
  Jacob, 13
Dobbins
  Jubale, 13
Dobson
  William, 10
Dodge
  J.R., Attorney, 33
  James R, 191
  James R., 191
  Jas A, 183
  Jas N, 186
  Jas. N, 186
Dolton
  David, 164
Doub
  John, 108

E

East
  Thos, 95
  Thos., 95
Eny[?]
  Abraham, 9
Enyart
  David, 70
Evans, 115, 118
  Isaac, 110, 111, 112, 113, 114, 115, 116, 117, 118
  Mr., 116, 118

F

Fair[**Fain**]
  McKeal, 179
Farmer
  Mrs., 171, 172
  Widow, 170, 171
Felts
  W[?], Sheriff, 186
  Wilie, Sheriff, 187
Feltz
  Wilie, Sheriff, 192
Fleming
  D.I., 192
Floyd
  John, Governor of Virginia, 65
Fogler
  Philip, 123, 125, 126
Forsyth
  Benjamin, 158
  Benjn, 159
  Benjn., 157
Forsythe
  Benjamin, 158, 159, 160, 161
Forsyths
  B, 157
Fowler
  T., 5
Foy
  Miles, 146, 147
  Mr Miles, 148
  Selena F.J., 146
Franklin
  S., 173
Free Persons of Color

Index

Bell
  John, 4, 5
  Nathan, 2, 3, 4, 5
  Nathan, taken up as a Runaway, 4
Fowler
  Tapley, 5, 6
  Taply, 5
Fowlers
  Tapley, 5
Franklin
  Stephen, 173
Gideon, 2. *See* Gideon, a yellow boy
Freeland
  John, 193
Frost
  Ezekiel, 164, 165
  James B., 165
  Jas B, 164
Frost's Iron Works, 165
Fulburt[?]
  Russ, 193

G

GA Counties
  Clarke, 123, 124, 125, 126, 127
  Lincoln, 110, 111, 114
GA Towns
  Augusta, 112
  Watkinsville, 124, 127
Garrat
  James, 189
Garret
  Wellcom, 103
  Wellcombe, 103
Garrett
  Welcome, 104
Gearhart
  Hiram, 100
  Leonard, 100, 101, 102
Gennett
  Thomas, 13, 32, 34, 45, 48, 59, 63
George
  Prestly, 139
  Prestly Sr., 139
Gettings
  Richard, 84
Gibson
  J, 157
  J.S., 2
  Jeremiah, 158, 159
  JH, 138
  John, 158
  Milly, 137, 138
  Mr Jeremiah, 157
  Patrick, 110, 117, 118
  Patrick, Esquire, 114, 118
  Patrick, JP, 113, 114, 115, 116, 117, 118
  W.N., JP, 44, 45, 52, 53, 143
  William N., Esquire, JP, 52
  William, Esquire, JP, 51
Giddans
  Margaret, 105
Giddings
  Margaret, 105
Gideon
  a yellow boy, 1
  Margaret, 99, 108
Gideons
  Margaret, 107, 109
  Mrs., 108
  Richard, 83
Gilbreaths, 142
Gileson
  William N., Esquire, 42, 44
Gillaspie
  Elijah, 95, 96, 97
Ginnett
  thomas, 33
  Thomas, 31, 35, 37, 40
Gitians
  Mrs, 106
  Mrs., 105, 106
Gittans
  Mrs., 106
Gittens
  Margaret, 80, 109
  Margt., 79
  Miss, 96, 97
Gittians
  Mrs., 106
Gittin
  Margaret, 90
Gitting
  Mrs., 85
Gittings
  Margaret, 83, 84, 89, 90, 91, 101
  Margeret, 91, 93, 96
  Mrs., 84, 85, 86, 87, 88, 91, 92, 93, 94, 95, 100, 101
  Richard, 84

Index

Roger, 84
Gittins
  M, 89
  Margaret, 83, 88, 89, 95, 98, 103, 104
  Miss, 96, 97
  Mrs., 98, 100
  Widow, 98
Glass
  Capt Dudley, 129, 131, 132
  Capt. Dudley, 130, 131
  Capt. Dudly, 128
  Dudley, 127, 128, 129, 130, 132
  Dudly, 131, 133
Glen
  Tyre, 184, 189
Golding
  Reuben, 68, 69
  Reubin D, 154
Gough
  John E., 182, 196
  Wm., 193
Grabs
  William, 107
Graves
  S., 178
Gray
  James, JP, 136
  Joseph, 186
Gross
  Calvin, 184, 194
Guilford Court House, 142
Guinn
  T.P., 163
  Thornton Preston, 163, 164
Gurhart
  Heriam, 100

H

Hadby
  Thos, JP, 97
  Thos., JP, 98
Hadly
  Thomas, 95
Haines
  Jonth, JP, 99
Hall
  Wm, 194
Hamflins
  John, 192
Hampton
  H.G., 183, 187
  HG, 185
  T.D., 193
  William W, 166
  William W., 166
  Wm W, 166
  Wm., 165
  Wm. W, 166
  Wm. W., 166, 167
Hanes
  James S., 188
Harding
  SB, 182
Hare
  R.O., 193
Harper
  John, 127, 129, 130
  Polly, 127
Harris
  Capt., 83, 84, 85, 86
Hauser, 106
  E.T., 193
  G, 102
  Geo, 99, 103, 109

  George, 83, 87, 88, 89, 90, 91, 93, 96, 97, 98, 103, 104, 105, 108, 109
  Michael, 102, 103, 107
  Michl., 107
  Mr., 92
  P., 103, 104
  Peter, 96, 102, 103
  Squire, 84, 91, 92, 93, 94
Hausers
  George, 97
Hauzer
  G, 79
  George, 79, 80, 81, 82
Hay[?]
  Ms, 168
Haynes
  I. Olen, 192
  James, 191
  Thos, 186
  W J Haynes, JP, 178
  WJ, JP, 178, 179
Helton
  Allen, 195, 196
Va Counties, 32
Hickman
  Anna, 166
  Edward, 90
  Miss Anna, 166
Hickmon
  Edwin, 90, 91, 92, 93
  William, 90, 91
Hikman
  Anna, 167
Hill

Index

Elizabeth, 129, 130
J.G., 139
James S., 139
Jas H., 138
Jas. S., 138
Jno., 5, 6
John, 179
M, 146
william, 132
William, 127, 128, 129, 130, 131, 132
Wm, 128
Wm., 128, 130, 131
Hines
  Ro, 171
Holcom
  Geo, Sheriff, 189, 190
Holcomb
  Drury, 80
  G, Sheriff, 185, 191
  G., 188
Hooper
  Elijah, 107
Hough
  Eph., 188
Houser
  G, 89
  Geo, 98
  George, 83, 89, 90, 95, 98, 101
  Mr., 98
  Squire, 100, 101
Hudspeth
  Airs, 12
  John, 10, 12, 70
Huffman
  H, 170
Hughes

  Mrs., 172
Hughs
  Matthew M., 98
  Nancy R., 172
Hunt
  John, 141
  Nathan, 193
  P, 185
Hutchens
  Giles, 193
  Sandy, 193

I

Ireland
  A, 187
  Albert, 191
Isbell
  Richard, 91
  Richd., 90, 92
Isbill
  Richard, 90, 91

J

James[**Jarvis**]
  Thomas, 175
Jarratt
  Isaac, 184
  J, 189, 192
Johnson
  C, 136
  Jas. T., 188
Jones
  B.F., 182
  H.C., 16, 19, 23, 27, 63, 68, 69
  H.C., Attorney, 14, 34, 43, 54, 55, 60, 74
  Hamilton C, 71

Hamilton C, Esquire, 73
Hamilton C., 73
Hamilton C., Attorney, 14, 62, 64
J.S., 182
Mr., 65
Mr. H.C., 65, 72
Mr. Hamilton C., 63
Patrick, 182
PM, Deputy Sheriff, 187
Jordan
  Daniel J, 149
  Edmund M, 149, 150, 151
  Edmund M, Guardian of Daniel J Jordan, 149
  Edmund M., 149
  James T, 149, 150, 151
  James T., 148, 149
  Seth A, 149
Jourdan
  Rowlan, 179
Joyce
  W.A., 183, 184, 185, 188, 190
  WA, 184, 187, 189, 191, 196, 198
  Will A., 191

K

Kelly
  L.D., 183, 193

Index

LD, 183, 184, 192
Kent[?]
  CG, 193
Kerby
  Jesse, 104
  Mr. Jesse, 104
Kernbough
  Nat., 182
Kerr
  John, 65, 66, 72
  Mr., 65
Kincannon
  Geo, JP, 106, 107
Kincanon
  George, JP, 105
Kinkenson[?] forge, 84
Kinnaman
  Saml., 108
Kinnamen
  Samuel, 108
Kinshaw
  Jonathan, 178
Kirby
  Jes, 103
  Jesse, 102, 103, 104
  Mr., 106
  Mr. Jesse, 102, 103
Kist
  Hy, 190
Kraubs
  William, 107

L

Ladd
  Thomas, 32, 35, 39, 46, 47, 49, 59
  Thos., Agent for Plaintiff, 37
Lafffoon
  Hardin, 187
Laffoon
  Hardin, 188
  Hardin S., 187
Lain
  David, 89, 90
Lard
  James, 117, 118
Lash
  Jacob, 107
Laugenour
  A.L., 182
Laurence
  Saml., 104
  Samuel, 104
Laurens
  Saml., 103
Laurenz
  Samuel, 103
Leard
  James, 117, 118
Lesters
  Jesse, 96
Lewis
  W.T., 73
  William, 7, 42
  William T, 76
  William T., 64, 76
Lilard
  John, 134
Lindsey
  Mathew, 193
Long
  Alfred, 185, 189
  Isaac, 188
  Isaac Senr., 182
  Thomas, 186
  W.W., 181, 190
  W.W., Sheriff, 184, 187
  WW, 185, 189, 191
  WW Esqr, 182
  WW, Sheriff, 184, 186
Longino
  John Thos, 12
  Tho, 96
  Thos, 95
Louis
  W.T., 61
  William Terel, 56, 57
Lugina
  Thomas, 108
Lynch
  Geog., 193
  George, 183

M

Mabanis, 141
Macay
  Spruce, 12
Mangum
  Willie P., 21
  Willie P., Judge, 18, 26
Marshal
  Henery, 193
Martin
  AW, 182
  E.L., 175, 177
  Edmund L., 149
  Gilligut, 193
  J.J., 5
  J.J. Esqr., 5
  James G, 152, 153

Index

James G., 151, 152, 153
Jane, 85
John J, 149
M.L., 193
Martha, 149
Mrs Martha, 149
Mrs. Martha, 149
T.S., 182, 185, 188, 189, 190, 191, 192
Thomas, 153
Thomas Esqr., 152
Thos., 153
TS, 183, 184, 187, 189, 196, 198
Matheson
  Higason, 110, 113
  Higgason, 114
Mathesons Ferry on Little River in Georgia, 114
Matlock
  John, 134
Matthews
  Tandy, 178
McBride
  W.W., 182
McCay
  Spruce, 10
McCraig
  Jacob, 106, 107
McCraw
  Jacob, 105
  Sandy, 127
McCreery
  W.W., Notary Public, 66

William W., Notary Public, 66
McDowell
  John, JP, 111, 113
McKiney
  Jesse, 83
  Mr, 2
McKinney
  Jesse, 86
  Jesse, JP, 87, 89
McKinny
  Jesse, 88, 104
  Jesse, Esquire, 104
  Jesse, JP, 90
Mckinsey
  Mr., 100
McKinsey, 100
  Thomas, 100, 101
Mcrery
  William W., 65
Melton
  Jonathan, 124, 125, 126, 127
Miller
  Matthew, 127
Milner
  Matthew, 130
Milton
  Jonathan, 123
Mitchel
  Mr., 92, 93
  W.A., 175
Mitchell, 100, 101
  Gideon, 103
  Mr, 106
  Mr., 105
  Robert, 102
  Robt., 101
Moody
  N, 142

Nathaniel, Constable, 143
Moor
  Matthew R., Esquire, 117
Moore
  Albert, 165
  Andrew, 141
  Greene, 164
  Matthew R., CC, 111
  Matthew R., CCC, 113, 118
  Matthew R., Clerk, 111, 113
  Matthew R., Esquire, 111, 113
  William C., 150
  Wm. C., 151
Morehead
  James T, Solicitor, 149
  Jas T, Solicitor, 148
Mosby
  James, 122
  James L., 119, 120
  JamesL., 119
  Jane, 119, 122, 123
  R.W., 119, 120
  Robert G, 120, 121
  Robert G., 119
  Robert W, 120, 121, 122
  Robert W., 119
  Robt G, 122
  Robt. W, 122

Index

William L., 119, 120
Wm L., 122
Mullato Child, 179
Myers
  B.C., 186, 187, 191
  BC, 187, 190

N

Nash
  F., Attorney, 74
  T, 122
Naylor
  Jo. R., 183
NC Counties
  Caswell, 63
  Iredell, 7, 13, 15, 18, 21, 22, 24, 26, 73
  Orange, 122, 140, 141
  Person, 63
  Rowan, 69
  Surry, 7, 10, 12, 13, 14, 15, 16, 19, 20, 21, 23, 24, 26, 27, 28, 30, 43, 45, 51, 52, 53, 68, 69, 70, 73, 74, 80, 83, 84, 88, 90, 91, 95, 99, 103, 105, 178
  Wilkes, 6, 7, 13, 41, 54, 55, 57
NC Towns
  Belews Creek, 179
  Bethania, 107
  Bethany, 102
  Crawford, 140, 146, 166, 167
  Danbury, 152, 153
  Germanton, 30, 31, 32, 36, 39, 41, 42, 43, 44, 45, 46, 48, 51, 52, 53, 55, 57, 58, 68, 69, 109, 111, 117, 158, 159, 165
  Germantown, 3
  Guilford, 142
  Hillsboro, 140, 141
  Milton, 63
  Rockford, 19, 23, 26, 27, 83, 89, 91, 96, 98, 104
  Rockford, Surry County, 15
  Salem, 4, 142
  Salisbury, 4, 76
  Statesville, 13, 19, 22
  Surry, 178
Neal
  Christopher, 2, 4
Negroes
  Negroes with African Marks on Temple & Face, 125
Nelson
  Isaac H., 146, 148
  John H., 146, 148
  William F., 146, 148
Nicholson
  Thomas A., 196

O

Odeneal, 112, 114, 118
  Jn., 115
  Jno, 110, 116
  Jno., 115
  John, 110, 111, 112, 113, 114, 115, 116, 117, 118
  Mr. John, 110
Odineal
  Mr. John, 117
Oriply
  Samuel, 110

P

Parks
  Jas., C.M.E, 79
  Jas., Clerk & Master, 91
  Jas., CM -Equity, 83
  Jas., CME, 91, 96
  Jos., CME, 89
ParksJas., CME, 83
Patterson
  Tho, 189
  Tyre, 192
Payne
  Robert, 150, 151
Pearce
  John, 66, 67
Pearson
  RM, 186
Perkins
  Mr., 88
  Thomas, 83, 88, 89, 91, 103, 104

Index

Thomas, Esquire, 104
Thomas, Jp, 91
Thomas, JP, 86, 87, 90, 93
Thoms, Esquire, 103
thos, JP, 88
Thos, JP, 89, 90, 92
Thos., 86, 105, 106
Thos., Esquire, 83
Thos., JP, 94, 95
Perrin
  Saml., 113
  Saml., JP, 113, 114, 115, 116, 117, 118
Perry
  John, 141
Pettiford
  Drury, 6
  Drury, a free man of color, 6
Philips
  Ed., 193
Phillips
  Benjamin, 193
  Ed, 183
  Edward, 192
  W.T., 190
Pleasants
  Saml., JP, 36, 38, 41, 60
  Samuel, 32, 34
  Samuel, Esquire, 36, 38
  Samuel, Esquire, JP, 58

Samuel, JP, 37, 39, 46, 47, 48, 49, 58
Poindexter
  Arch., 183
  Archibald, 183, 193
  Jno. F., Attorney, 147
  RC, 182
Poor
  Caty, 90
  Robert, 83, 87, 88
Poore
  Catey, 91
  Caty, 90, 93, 94
  Mrs., 93
  Robert, 83, 90, 91, 95, 96
Presley
  Dr. Saml., 113
Presly
  Dr. Saml., 114, 116
Pressly
  Samuel, 116
Pucket
  Richard, 105
  Richd, 104
Puckett
  Richard, 104
  Richd, 105, 107
  Richd., 106
  Thos M, 139
Puryear
  R.C., 190
  RC, 193

R

Rainey

William, 116, 117, 118
Rainy
  William, 118
  Wm., 118
Rand
  W, 167
  Wm., 167
Raney
  William, 117
  Wm., 113, 114
Rank
  Gottlib, 107
Ranke
  Gottleb, 107
Reaves
  George, 128
Reavis
  George, 127
  Joseph, 189
  Peter, 127
Reece
  A, 187
  Hadly, 178
  John, 196
  Sarah, 196
Reese
  Hadly, 178
Reeves
  HH, 170
Reinhart
  Christian, Jr., 188
Removal of Slaves, 121
Reney
  Wm., 115
Reves
  Peter, 128, 130, 131, 132, 133
Rey
  William S, 152
Rice
  T., 11

Index

Richardson
  Wm. H., 65
Rierson
  James, 147
  James Senr., 147
  Jos., 148
Rine
  Will O, 190
Rivers
  Flat River, 141
Roberts
  Joshua, 95, 96, 97
  Priscilla, 95, 96, 97
  Pryscilla, 97
Robinson
  A, 158, 164
  A[?], 159
Rominger
  Joseph, 2
  Martin, 2
Rose
  Hugh, 134
  Philip, 134, 135
  Thomas, 134, 135
Roughton
  E.C., Deputy Sheriff, 183
  EC, Deputy Sheriff, 184
Roya
  Eliz, 102
Royal
  C, 183, 192
Royer
  Elisabeth, 103
Ruffin
  Thomas, 3, 4, 122
Runaway Slave, 4
Rutledge
  E., Deputy Sheriff, 30, 33, 73

Rutlege
  E., Deputy Sheriff, 54, 55, 60

S

Sale[?]
  Wm, 189
Salmon
  Jacob, 159
Salmons
  Jacob, 158
Saunders
  C.H., 121, 123
  CH, 122
  Chancellor H, 123
  Chancellor H., 119
SC Districts
  Abbeville, 110, 113, 114, 115, 117, 118
SC Towns
  Charleston, 124, 125
  Vienna, 112
Scot
  Gabriel, 56
  Jane, 9, 42, 56, 57
  Jemima, 77
  Jesse, 44, 45
  Jin, 44
  Jin, Malvina, Polly & Sally, 45
  Kiseah, 56
  Malvina, 44
  Mima, 44

  Mima, Wife of John a slave, 45
  Mima, Wife of John a Slave, 44
  Polly, 44
  Sal, 56
  Sally, 44
  Sam, 45
  Sillar, 56
Scott
  Edie, 67
  Free Nan, 62
  Gemima, 31
  Happy, 10
  J., 14, 18
  Jane, 13, 56, 61, 68, 69, 70, 71, 75
  Jane or free Jin, 70
  Jane, free woman of color, 7
  Jean, 10
  Jemima, 7, 10, 11, 13, 15, 16, 19, 20, 26, 27, 28, 29, 30, 31, 42, 43, 44, 50, 54, 55, 56, 58, 60, 61, 62, 63, 64, 65, 66, 68, 69, 70, 71, 72, 73, 74, 76
  Jemima, a free person, 74
  Jesse, 14, 15, 16, 17, 18, 31, 34, 38, 39, 42, 43, 47, 50, 51, 54, 55, 57, 60, 66, 68, 72, 74, 76

218

Index

Jin, 32, 35, 36, 37, 38, 39, 40, 46, 47, 49, 59, 60, 62
Karanhapuc, 70
Keziah, 10
Kiziah, 12, 70
Kiziah, a mulatto girl, 12
Malvina, 14, 22, 34, 35, 41, 48, 49, 50, 51, 52, 53, 54, 56, 60, 66, 74
Malvina:, 55
Mary, 66
Melvina, 13, 23, 24, 25, 26, 72, 73, 76
Mima, 31, 32, 34, 39, 43, 44, 45, 46, 47, 51, 52, 53, 54, 61
Mima against Badgett, 61
Mima or Jemima, 58
Nan, 35, 37, 40, 46, 48, 49, 59, 62
Nan, free born, 38
Nan, free woman of color, 33
Presilla, 10
Sall, 12
Sall, a mulatto girl, 12
Salley, 19
Sally, 18, 19, 20, 21, 22, 31, 32, 34, 36, 37, 41, 43, 44, 45, 50, 54, 55, 60, 72, 74, 76
Sarah, 10
Tin[?], 13
Scotts
  Jane, 61
  Jin, 38, 40, 59
Seals
  AM, 149
Settle
  Thos., 64
Sheaks
  John, 195
Shoars
  Wilie, 192
Shober
  Em, 174
  Emanuel, Clerk & Master in Equity, 100
  Emanuel, CME, 100, 102, 103, 104, 108, 109, 110
  Eml, Clerk & Master in Equity, 110
  G, 140, 141, 174
  G, JP, 141, 142
  G., 174
  Gottlieb, 174
Shoope
  Samuel, 107
Shore
  Wesley, 193
Sillivan
  Richard, 44
Simmon
  Sterne, Senr., 112
Simmons
  John, 110, 111, 112, 113, 114
  Stern, 110
  Stern, Junr., 110
  Stern, Senr., 110, 111
  Sterne, 113
  Sterne, Junr., 111, 112, 113
  Sterne, Senr., 111
Sintz[?]
  L., 182
Slater
  F., 63
Slave
  George, 112
  Jin, 8
Slave Patrol District
  Deep Creek, Yadkin County, 191
Slave Patrol Districts
  Baltimore, Yadkin County, 183, 184, 189, 190, 192, 193
  Bean Shoal, Yadkin County, 189, 192
  Chinquepen, Yadkin County, 193
  Chinquepin, Yadkin County, 192
  Deep Creek, Yadkin County, 184, 186, 192, 193, 194
  East Bend, Yadkin County, 193

Index

Hampton, Yadkin County, 188
Hamptonville, Yadkin County, 182, 188, 191, 193
Huntsville, Yadkin County, 181, 185, 186, 189, 190, 193
Jonesville, Yadkin County, 183, 185, 187, 188, 190, 193
Knoles, Yadkin County, 184, 194
Panther Creek, Yadkin County, 182
Speers, Yadkin County, 187, 191
Yadkin, Yadkin County, 182
Yadkinville, Yadkin County, 183, 184, 185, 189, 192, 193
Slave Patroll Districts
Huntsville, Yadkin County, 189
Slavery
Ilegal State of, 76
Unjust, 76
Slaves
Aaron, 154

Abe, 154, 169, 170
Abel, 143
Abram, 149, 150
Adain, 159
Adair, 158
African Negro Dick, 126
Aggy, 163
Alford, 163
Alfred, 146, 148, 197
Amelia, 149, 150
Anderson, 146, 148, 197
Andy, 154
Anna, 146, 148
Ben, 134
Bet, 197
Bett, 86
Betty, 170
Bob, 139, 140
Bob, Beating Prestly George, 139
Brittania, 120, 122
Brittannia, 122
Calvin, 195
Celia, 137, 138
Charity, 163
Charles, 158, 159, 161
Clark, 177
Cloe, 119, 120, 122, 123
Collen, 169, 170
Cora, 146, 148
Cornelia, 146, 148
Cr[?]asa, a Runaway, 167
Cynthia, 154

Daniel, 154, 169, 170
Danl, 169
Dick, 125, 126
Dick, Absconded or Runaway, 126
Dick, African Negro, 124, 126
Dicy, 170
Dilcy, 170
Dolly, 149, 150
Eliz, 150
Eliza, 149, 154, 170
Elly, 149, 150
Enoch, 174
Esther, 152, 153
exemptions from taxation, 177
Fanny, 158, 166, 197
Floyd, 146
Franky, 169, 170
Franny, 159
Gabriel, 7
Gabril, 42
George, 112, 114, 115, 116, 118
Haggar, 170
Hanah, 154, 170
Handy, 197
Hannah, 169
Happy, 7
Harry, 149, 165
Henry, 149, 150
Jack, 163
Jefferson, 195
Jeney, 154
Jennet, 154
Jennett, 154
Jenny, 154, 164

Index

Jeny, 8
Jerry, 134
Jim, 170
Jo, 146
John, 44, 45, 52, 53, 119, 180
John Shull, 173
John[?], 123
Jordan, 154
Joseph, 148
Judith, 146
Julia, 149, 150
Kisiah, 42
Lewis, 154, 169, 170, 177
Liza, 169, 170
Louisa, 146, 148
Lucey, 163
Lucille, 154
Lucinda, 197
Lucy, 143, 169, 170
Mahali, 177
Manual, 154
Manuel, 169, 170
Margaret, 146, 148
Maria, 143, 152
Mariah, 152, 153
Martha, 149, 151, 154
Mary, 146, 148, 151, 154
May, 149
Milly, 197
Moses, 86
Nathan, 146, 148
Nelson, 143
Patrick, 143
Patt, 163
Permits to sell produce, 177
Peter, 140, 141

Peter, Runaway, 141
Peter, Stealing a Mare, 141
philis, 195
Phillis, 178
Pleasant, 149, 150
Raymond, 154
Rebecca, 146, 148
Sal, 7, 42
Sally, 146, 148
Sam, 142, 143, 179
Sam, Threatening C.L. Banner, 142
Samuel, 149, 150
Sarah, 157, 160
Scott, 149, 151
Silas, 138
Sillar, 7, 42
Silvy, 158
Stephen, 154
Sterling, 154
Susan, 154
Synthia, 154
Temperance, 196
Tisbey, 128, 129, 130, 131, 132, 133
Washington, 180
Wassar, 134
Wiley, 154
Wilie, 154
Will, 146
Winney, 133
Smith
E.D., 194
Ed, 184
Irby, 62
Joseph, JP, 136

Mr., 61
Mr. Irby, 61
Snow
Jordan, 194
Snow[?]
Henry, 193
Spears
Samuel B, 193
Speer
S.T., Sheriff, 181
Samuel, 30
Stanter
Francis, 107
States
Georgia, 110, 111, 114, 123, 124
Ohio, 65
Pennsylvania, 101, 105
South Carolina, 4, 110, 112, 113, 114, 115, 117, 118, 124
Tennessee, 50, 133, 134, 135
Virginia, 2, 4, 5, 13, 31, 32, 33, 34, 36, 37, 39, 46, 47, 48, 50, 55, 58, 60, 61, 62, 63, 64, 65, 66, 72, 102, 119, 128, 129, 130, 131, 132, 163
Steelman
Charles, 72
Jackson, 193
Jno, 189
John, 185
Joseph, 193
William, 185

Index

Wm., 193
Steelmon
  Charles, 30
  Mr., 30
Steyer
  Henry, 4
Steyer[?]
  Henry, 3
Stinson
  Isaac, 191
Stone
  S., Sheriff, 2, 71
Stovall
  Jos., 123
Stroud
  William, 123
  Wm., JP, 127
Sugart
  L.L., 193
Sullivan
  Richard, 42, 43, 44, 45, 51, 52, 53
  Richd., 43
  Rt., 9
  W, 170
Superior Court of Salisbury District, 74
Suttle
  Reuben, 6, 7, 8, 13, 41, 42, 54, 55, 56, 57
  reuben, Sr., 54
  Ruben, 41

T

Talbert
  John, 5
Talbut
  John, 5
Taliaferro
  Charles, JP, 90
  Chas., JP, 92, 93, 94, 95
Taliefero
  Charles, JP, 91
Talman
  John, 66, 67, 68
Tate
  Huriah, 140, 141, 142
  Jephania, 140
  Uriah, 141
Taylor
  Saml. H., 138, 139
  Samuel H., 138
Terrentines Quarter, 141
Thomas
  Wray, 35, 39, 59, 65
  Wray, Agent for Defendant, 37
  Wray, Attorney, 64
Thompson
  Thos., JP, 101, 102
Thomson
  AH, 184
Tilley
  David, 173
TN Counties
  Stuart, 133, 135, 136
TN Towns
  Dover, 136
Todd
  James E., JP, 111, 113
Tomlin
  A.N., 183
  AN, 185
Town Fork Place, Stokes County, 170
Tramel
  Thomas, 123
Trammel
  Thomas, 124, 126, 127
Transou
  Abraham, 107
  Abram, 107
Transu
  P., JP, 71
Transue
  Peter, 69
Trewett
  William, 113, 114
Truett
  Wm., 114
Truitt
  William, 110
  Williams, 115
  Wm., 115
  Wms., 115
Tucker
  Benjamin C, Guardian of Martha E Tucker, 152
  Benjamin C., 152
  Benjn. C., 153
  Gabriel H, 152
  Gabriel H., 152, 153
  James B, 152
  Martha E, 152
  Martha E., 152, 153
Tuttle
  P., 2
  Peter, 1

Index

U

Unthank
  Jona., 87
  Jonath, 103
  Jonathan, 83, 87, 103, 104, 105
  William, 104

V

VA Counties
  Cumberland, 42
  Fairfax, 4, 5
  Franklin, 100, 102
  Halifax, 62, 63, 127, 128, 129, 130, 131, 132, 163
  Henrico, 13, 31, 32, 33, 34, 36, 37, 39, 46, 47, 49, 55, 58, 60, 61, 62, 72
  Powhatan, 119, 120, 122
VA Towns
  Alexandria, 4
  City of Richmond, 13, 33
  Clear Mount, 2
  Henrico, 47
  Richmond, 64, 65, 66, 72
Vanestor[?]
  Wm L., 190
Vanhoy
  Mr. John Esqr., 179

Vest
  Samuel, 107, 108
Vestal
  Isaac, 188
  Martha, 196

W

Wainscott family, 70
Wall
  Robert, 150, 151
Walsh
  J., 41
  J. JP, 56
  J., Esquire, 41
  J., JP, 42, 55, 56
  Jn., 57
  Jn., JP, 8, 57, 58
  John, 55, 56
Watkins
  Frans., 123
  Samuel, 63
Watson
  Benja, 10
Welch
  John Esqr., 6
Welfare
  P.V., 182
Well[?]ten
  Alfred, 188
West
  James, 188, 191, 193
Whitaker
  William, 185
Wilbourne
  Richard, 64
Wilburn
  Edmund, 191
Williams
  C.W., 192, 197, 198

Capt., 124
Col
  Joseph, 43
  Col., 9, 44, 45, 52, 53
  Col. Jos., 44, 52
  Col. Joseph, 45, 52, 53, 61, 70
  Col., overseer, 45
  CW, 192, 193, 198
  CW, Guardian of William Beren, 198
  FR, 194
  Hardy, 188
  Isaac, 192
  J, 182, 191
  J., 50
  Jn L., 193
  Jo, 10, 11, 12, 61, 65, 73, 185, 186, 193
  Jo, C.S.C., 19, 21, 25
  Jo, Clerk, 27
  Jo, Clk, 17
  Jo, CSC, 23, 27, 29
  Jos, 182
  Jos., Jr., 53
  Joseph, 7, 10, 11, 12, 13, 14, 15, 17, 21, 25, 29, 33, 50, 61, 64, 68, 69, 72, 74, 75, 76, 191, 193
  Joseph Jr., 44
  Joseph Junr., 62, 63
  Joseph, Agent for Lewis

223

Index

Williams, 17, 25
Joseph, Clerk, 23, 25, 28
Joseph, Clerk of Court, 19
Joseph, Jr., 52
Lewis, 14, 15, 16, 17, 18, 19, 20, 21, 22, 23, 24, 25, 26, 27, 28, 29, 30, 31, 32, 33, 34, 35, 36, 37, 39, 41, 42, 43, 44, 45, 46, 47, 48, 49, 50, 51, 52, 53, 54, 55, 56, 57, 58, 60, 61, 62, 63, 64, 65, 66, 68, 69, 71, 72, 73, 74, 76, 77
M.C., 190
Maj. Jos., 43
Mr. Joseph, 13, 62
Mr. Joseph, Agent of Lewis Williams, 43
Mr. Lewis, 33, 54, 55, 60
N.L., 28
Nathaniel, 10
Nicholas, 23, 27
Nicholas L., 16, 20, 24, 28
NL, 16, 20, 24

Rob, 159
Rob., 124
Robert, 124
Robt., 124, 158
Thos., 182, 193
WS, 182
Williamson
  Elizabeth, 164
Willow
  B.F., 175
Wilson
  H.C., 193
  HC, 183, 192
Winston
  Jos, 10, 11
  Joseph, 11
Wood
  Francis, 187, 188
  Mr., 9
Woodridge
  Wm., 12
Woodruff
  John J., 185
Woodson
  R.J., 123
Woodward
  Aaron, 123, 124, 125, 127
Wooldridge
  Gibson, 12
  William, 12
Woolridge
  William, 12
Word
  Col., 84, 86
  Mr., 93
  Thomas A, 80

Thomas A., 80
Thos A., 98
Wright
  Tho B, 23
  Tho B, Sheriff, 23, 24, 27, 28, 55, 60
  Tho B., Sheriff, 20, 54, 60
  Tho. B., Sheriff, 14, 15, 16, 19, 20, 33
  Thos. B., 20
  Thos. B., Sheriff, 20, 30, 73
  Thos. B., Sheriff of Surry County, 16
  Thos., Sheriff, 73

Y

Yarrel
  Thomas, 102
Yarrell
  Thomas, 102

Z

Zachary
  Danl., 194
Ziglar
  William M., 175
  Wm., 175

ABOUT THE AUTHORS

WILLIAM L. BYRD, III has been involved in genealogical and historical research for more than thirty years. His primary areas of interest are Native Americans, African Americans, West Indians, East Indians and Moors in Virginia, North Carolina, and South Carolina.

He has been published by the *North Carolina Genealogical Society Journal*, the *Magazine of Virginia Genealogy*, *The Rowan County Register*, and *The South Carolina Magazine of Ancestral Research*. He has also co-authored articles with Sheila Stover in the *North Carolina Genealogical Society Journal*, *The Augustan Society Omnibus*, the *Pan-American Indian Association News*, and the *Eagle: New England's American Indian Journal*. He has received an "Award of Special Recognition" from The North Carolina Society of Historians in the category of "The History Article Award" for preserving North Carolina history.

He is a U.S. Army Veteran from the Vietnam era, and served with the U.S. Armed Forces overseas. He is currently retired, and resides with his family in Hickory, North Carolina.

ᛜ ᛝ

JOHN H. SMITH holds a BA in psychology from Lenoir Rhyne College, and did his graduate work at Winthrop University. His professional memberships include American Psychological Association, and Phi Alpha Theta (National Honor Society in History.) In addition to his full-time career, Mr. Smith is a part-time continuing education instructor of genealogy and family history, and a part-time research assistant to Catawba County Historical Association.

Mr. Smith was the editor of *The Burke Journal* (1992-1995), a quarterly publication of the Burke County Genealogical Society, (winner of the *Excellence in Periodical Publishing Award* from the North Carolina Genealogical Society, 1995.) He has presented numerous programs to genealogical groups in North Carolina in the past fifteen years, and has twice been a speaker at the South Carolina Genealogical Society's summer workshop. His articles have been published in *The Burke Journal*, *Catawba Cousins*, the *Rowan Register*, the *South Carolina Magazine of Ancestral Research* and several other local/county quarterlies.

Other Heritage Books by William L. Byrd, III:

Against the Peace and Dignity of the State: North Carolina Laws Regarding Slaves, Free Persons of Color, and Indians

Bladen County, North Carolina Tax Lists: 1768 through 1774, Volume I

Bladen County, North Carolina Tax Lists: 1775 through 1789, Volume II

For So Long as the Sun and Moon Endure: Indian Records from the North Carolina General Assembly Sessions, & Other Sources

In Full Force and Virtue: North Carolina Emancipation Records, 1713-1860

North Carolina General Assembly Sessions Records: Slaves and Free Persons of Color, 1709-1789

North Carolina Slaves and Free Persons of Color: Chowan County, Volume One

North Carolina Slaves and Free Persons of Color: Chowan County, Volume Two

North Carolina Slaves and Free Persons of Color: Pasquotank County

North Carolina Slaves and Free Persons of Color: Perquimans County

Villainy Often Goes Unpunished: Indian Records from the North Carolina General Assembly Sessions, 1675-1789

Other Heritage Books by William L. Byrd, III and John H. Smith:

North Carolina Slaves and Free Persons of Color: Burke, Lincoln, and Rowan Counties

North Carolina Slaves and Free Persons of Color: Hyde and Beaufort Counties

North Carolina Slaves and Free Persons of Color: Iredell County

North Carolina Slaves and Free Persons of Color: Mecklenburg, Gaston, and Union Counties

North Carolina Slaves and Free Persons of Color: McDowell County

North Carolina Slaves and Free Persons of Color: Stokes and Yadkin Counties

www.ingramcontent.com/pod-product-compliance
Lightning Source LLC
Chambersburg PA
CBHW071711160426
43195CB00012B/1644